Any Objections?

Objections to the Gospel Answered

By John D. Legg

Covenant Books UK

COVENANT BOOKS UK (CBUK)
10 Kelsey Close, Liss. GU33 7HR
Email: office@covenantbooksuk.org.uk
Website: https://covenantbooksuk.org.uk/
© John D. Legg, David W. Legg 2007, 2022

First published by Evangelical Press in 1994, and now by Covenant Books UK in 2022.

Created in *LibreOffice Community* 7.3.3.2 with open source software running on *Fedora 36 Linux*.

First published by CBUK in 2022. ISBN: 9798832372334

The aim of this book is to remove some of the obstacles to accepting the Christian faith. It is a book for those who have a genuine problem, a real question, or a relevant issue to which they need an answer.

John Legg sets out answers to a wide range of objections so that the way may be cleared for the honest reader to take the next step of truly accepting the gospel of the Lord Jesus Christ.

This book will also prove valuable to believers who are preparing themselves to answer objections raised by their friends, colleagues or family.

After ministering for over 40 years in Yorkshire and Shrewsbury, John D. Legg retired to Cardiff. He and his wife Beryl have four children and eleven grandchildren. His previously published books include:

- *The King and His Kingdom* (Matthew's gospel, *Welwyn Commentary*, EP Books);

- *The Church that Christ Built* (Church History, EP Books);

- *Serving as a Deacon* (Covenant Books UK)

- *When We Don't Understand* (Jonah, Habakkuk, EP Books);

- *The Trinity and Us* (Covenant Books UK)

- *Dear Tom* and *Dear Beth* (Covenant Books UK)

- *The Gospel According to Elisha* (Covenant Books UK)

Contents

1.
Clearing the ground

The aim of this book is to remove some obstacles to accepting the Christian faith, referred to in the title as simply 'The Gospel'[1]. Before we embark on that, I want to clear the ground a little, so that we do not waste our time by being at cross-purposes. In other words, I want to make clear what I am trying to do and also what I am not trying to do.

First, I am aware that sometimes questions are raised merely in an attempt to divert the one who is pressing the claims of Christ on a rather unwilling hearer. That sort of objector will find little in this book to interest him. I am only concerned with those who have a genuine problem, a real question, a relevant issue to which they need an answer.

Secondly, there are many difficulties that people have which need not, and will not, concern us. They are not, as it were, life-threatening; they do not concern the essentials of the gospel[1] of Christ; one can become a Christian without having them settled.

Thirdly, I am not engaged in an intellectual exercise—in answering questions for their own sake. The assumption of this book is that if your problem is solved, if your question is answered and your objection dealt with, then you will in all honesty take the next step and trust Christ for yourself. Jesus himself said that only if someone were willing to do God's will, would he come to know the truth (John 8:31-32). God does not play games with people. Jesus also said that if we seek we will find (Luke 11:9). The sincere enquirer will not be disappointed.

Fourthly, although the subjects dealt with cover a wide range I do not flatter myself that every possible objection has been

---

1   The word 'Gospel' means 'good news', i.e., the good news of Jesus Christ. See Mark 1:1.

addressed. Nevertheless, these do show the way forwards. They indicate the method of dealing with other issues and answering other objections. In particular, they clarify the basic matters which may, in turn, render further questions superfluous.

Fifthly, these questions are not artificial ones. I have found that the 'put-up job', the question raised by a friend in order to get a discussion going, does not usually do any good. The questions we shall consider have all been raised with me in conversations, some of them many times. People really do have these difficulties and do need answers.

Sixthly, you will notice as we proceed that all the answers come from the Bible. I make no apology for this. Part of the justification for it will appear as we go along. But essentially the reason is that there is no other sure foundation. Apart from the Bible neither I nor anyone else can help. There is no other source of truth. God's word is my authority and must be yours too, if you hope to have certainty. I would not want to rely on my own wisdom, and I do not expect you to do so either!

2.
'I don't think it matters what you believe.'

Many people think that as long as you call yourself a Christian it's all right. They act as if it were permissible to define Christianity any way they like. They adopt a method that they would not think of using in ordinary life. For example, mathematical and scientific terms are clearly defined; you cannot use words like 'divide' or 'temperature' just as you wish. With the Christian faith, however, it seems that everything changes. 'I think' or 'I can't believe' become authoritative statements; the historic meanings of words and the basics of biblical truth disappear before our eyes. This will not do. It is not even common sense, let alone sound theology.

Have Christians always believed just what they wanted? Is Christianity simply vague—an empty container that you may fill as you prefer? How can we decide what Christianity really is? One legitimate method would be to consider the first historic use of the word '*Christian*': '*The disciples were called Christians first at Antioch*' (Acts 11:26). They did not claim the name; it was given to them because they had certain characteristics which marked them off from their neighbours. It was not at all vague. In the surrounding verses it is made perfectly clear that one has to become a Christian, that a Christian is a committed disciple of Jesus Christ, hence the nickname 'Christian'. Faith in him as Lord as well as Saviour is required; this is the result of the grace of God. Christian people meet together as the church of Jesus Christ. Many false ideas of Christianity—some of which we shall consider at greater length later—are immediately removed by this simple and logical method.

Jesus the Messiah's own definition

However, it may be claimed that words can change their meaning over the years, as some indeed do, so I want to go back even further, to the words of the founder, Jesus Christ himself. His words must be authoritative for all succeeding ages. All who claim to be his disciples must accept his definition. After his resurrection Jesus spent some time teaching his disciples further, preparing them for their work after he had left them. I will quote the passage for ease of reference:

He said to them, 'This is what I told you while I was still with you: everything must be fulfilled that is written about me in the Law of Moses, the Prophets and the Psalms.'

[45] Then he opened their minds so they could understand the Scriptures. [46] He told them, 'This is what is written: the Messiah will suffer and rise from the dead on the third day, [47] and repentance for the forgiveness of sins will be preached in his name to all nations, beginning at Jerusalem. [48] You are witnesses of these things. [49] I am going to send you what my Father has promised; but stay in the city until you have been clothed with power from on high.' (Luke 24:44-49)

In this passage we can see certain elements of the Christian faith, basic ideas which we must accept. We cannot believe what we like; we cannot pick and choose.

We will refer back to these Bible verses in the remainder of this chapter.

The religion of the book

First, it is obvious that Jesus appeals to the authority of the Bible —'*the Scriptures*'. He regards the Bible as true. He treats its prophecies as infallible (v.44)—they must be *fulfilled*—and he uses them to interpret his own death and resurrection (v.46). All through his life and ministry he had adopted the same procedure.

'*It is written*'[2] was the final answer to many a debate. '*The Scripture cannot be set aside*'[3] was his crushing retort to those Pharisees who argued with him. Now he shows the disciples that they are to continue in the same way. Christianity is to be the religion of the book.

It is the Old Testament to which Jesus is referring here, but his reference to the gift from the Father (v.49) takes us forward to the New Testament. The Holy Spirit, he had already told them, '*will teach you all things and will remind you of everything I have said to you*' (John 14:26). A little later he added, '*When he, the Spirit of truth, comes, he will guide you into all the truth*' (John 16:13). Thus, provision was made for the New Testament, which, through the work of the Holy Spirit, accurately records the teaching of Christ and his apostles.

The inescapable fact is that Christ regarded his 'religion' as based on the Bible. And this is what many object to. However, if it is Christianity you want and not some modern substitute, it is to the Bible that you must look. We have to submit to God's authority in the Scriptures. We have to admit that we cannot know these things ourselves; we must submit our ideas to his revelation.

Christ crucified and raised

Secondly, the Christian message is rooted in history; the gospel is based on actual events. This is one reason why the original 'Gospels' were accounts of the life and ministry of Jesus Christ, especially his death and resurrection, not just his teaching. He saved people by what he was and by what he did. He did not merely give us some help and encouragement in order to save ourselves. We must, therefore, believe the facts and also accept his explanation of their meaning. Some of this interpretation is found in these verses, Luke 24:44-49.

2   Matthew 4:4 and many other places.
3   John 10:35

Thirdly, then, we must accept what the Bible tells us about Jesus. It is not sufficient to say, 'But I have always regarded Jesus as just a good man and a wonderful teacher.' We have not been left to speculate in the dark. The Bible tells us clearly who he is and what he did. In this passage we are told that Jesus is '*the Messiah*' (v.46). Originally, and as used here, it was a title. It meant '*the Anointed One*', the Greek equivalent of the Hebrew '*Messiah*' is '*Christ*'. Christ is not a surname, like Smith, as we often use it nowadays. Prophets, priests and especially kings were anointed with oil, which represented the Holy Spirit being poured out on them to enable them to perform their God-given work. So Jesus is declared to be God's Anointed and appointed King and Saviour.

Although the Jewish leaders did not recognise it, the Bible tells us that this Messiah/Christ was to be divine. The New Testament makes it clear that Jesus, the Christ, was the '*Son of the living God*'[4]. We are concerned, not with a mere man, but with God made man, sometimes referred to as 'the God-man'. In fact, there is a hint of that even in v.47. The fact that the gospel was to be preached '*in his name*' can only mean that he himself is God. For the Jews, as these men were, no other name gave such authority and power. We can see the same use of the word in the command to baptise, given at the end of Matthew's Gospel. Baptism was to be administered '*in the name*'—a single name —'*of the Father and of the Son and of the Holy Spirit*' (Matthew 28:19).

Again, these verses tell us about the work of Christ in his death and resurrection. In fact the word used is not 'die' but '*suffer*' (Acts 24:46), telling us that Christ's death was not just a human event, a tragedy or mere example, but a sacrifice. As foreshadowed by the Old Testament law and prophecies, Jesus Christ came into the world with a specific mission. He had been given a people and came into the world to save them. According to Matthew 1:21, he was given the name *Jesus*, meaning 'God

---

4   For example, Matthew 16:16.

saves', because *'he will save his people from their sins.'* He did this by dying in their place and taking upon himself God's anger and punishment for them.

It is significant that when people ignore the Bible's own explanation of the cross, they cannot understand it at all. They see only tragedy and failure; they have no idea why Christians refer to the day on which he died as Good Friday!

The resurrection is also stated as a fact, a concrete historical fact. The record of the Gospels, reflected here, is that the tomb was empty and, indeed, had to be empty. The resurrection was the proof that all that Jesus had claimed was true: his deity, his innocence, his messiahship, and the fact that his death was planned as a sacrifice for sin. The resurrection declared with certainty that he had done what God had sent him to do, the sacrifice had been accepted, and his people would be saved. It also confirmed that one day, as he had said, he would return to judge the world (Acts 17:31).

We are not free to substitute our own idea of the resurrection, to suit perhaps our own denial of the supernatural. Saying that the disciples had a sense that Jesus was still with them, for example, neither fits the facts nor fulfils the function that the Bible ascribes to the resurrection. We cannot believe what we want on this topic either. If we remove all that offends people, we end up with nothing worth having.

Conversion and commitment

Fourthly, according to Jesus the message to be preached must demand that radical change of mind, heart and life which is called *'repentance'* (Luke 24:47). Sometimes, as here, the word *'repentance'* is used as the equivalent of 'conversion'; so, both faith and a radical change of mind are included in its meaning. Becoming a Christian involves more than just a mental acceptance of the truth of the message. There has to be a commitment to Christ, a commitment that includes personal trust in Christ as Saviour and a radical turning from the old life towards God and a new life.

Such a message will arouse opposition from men and women who do not want to change. They would, perhaps, like to have forgiveness and comfort; they would like to go to heaven when they die; they would like hope and joy and peace—but they like their old life even more. So they redefine Christianity: 'I don't think you have to take it all so seriously.' On the contrary, Jesus constantly asserted that wholehearted commitment was essential. He urged prospective disciples to '*estimate the cost*' of following him (Luke 14:28). If someone became his disciple he would have to '*deny*' himself, that is, say 'No' to his own sinful desires. He would have to '*take up his cross*', that is, be prepared to suffer for the sake of Christ (Matthew 16:24). Repentance is no easy change of opinion, but a complete reversal of our loyalties and priorities.

Some people's 'gospels' do not mention repentance. There is an 'easy-believe-ism' which omits it, and never mentions the cost of being a Christian. Later, as Christ's parable of the sower illustrates (Matthew 13:20-21), these people discover what is involved and give up their profession of faith. It was not real faith in the beginning. True believers persevere by God's grace.

Others take the deception (a hard word, but that is what it is) even further by promising a life of constant happiness and peace. Life will be a bed of roses—without the thorns. Coming to Christ immediately solves all your problems. Some even promise 'health and wealth' in the so-called 'prosperity gospel'. You should avoid these misleading ideas like the plague!

Good news

Fifthly, the apostles are commanded to promise '*the forgiveness of sins*' (Luke 24:47). This, you might think, would not cause any problems. Yet it does, for people do not like to think that they need mercy or that God only forgives some. They want to believe in a universal amnesty for all offenders. Indeed, they are encouraged in this by the clergy, of many denominations, who tell the congregations at funerals that everyone goes to heaven. There is no wrath of God, no judgement, no hell. Now this is an easy way to avoid objections from the people of the world. Everyone wants to believe that all are saved.

However, even from our own experience, we know that real reconciliation is impossible unless there is a genuine acceptance of guilt and a request for forgiveness. Apart from repentance and faith there is no forgiveness, and without knowing the gospel there will be no faith. For *'faith comes from hearing the message, and the message is heard through the word about Christ'* (Romans 10:17). Again this is not popular, but the proper response is not to deny it, but to make every effort to ensure that the good news is made known *'to all nations'* (Luke 24:47). Hence, this book.

God's power at work

Finally, the disciples are required in Luke 24:49 to wait in Jerusalem for the Father's gift to them. This is the gift of the Holy Spirit. Why do they have to wait? Because, apart from the work of the Holy Spirit, people cannot even believe. Their inability is not limited to their failure to be good enough for God. They cannot even receive a free gift; they cannot turn in repentance and faith.

The Holy Spirit, said Jesus, would *'prove the world to be in the wrong about sin and righteousness and judgement'* (John 16:8). Apart from his work we are spiritually blind and deaf. We cannot hear properly; we cannot understand properly, and are unable to submit to God (1 Corinthians 2:14; Romans 8:7). We are helpless. That is why Jesus told Nicodemus that he had to be born again[5], if he were even to see the kingdom of God. This is a term which has been debased in recent days by advertising agents and superficial evangelists, so we must be clear what is

5   Or, *'born from above'*, John 3:3,7

really meant. Being born again is not something that follows after people believe. On the contrary, it is essential for them if they are to believe in the first place. Without this work of the Holy Spirit they are 'dead' spiritually. Only when this has taken place can people think, understand, feel and respond to God properly. And this, said Jesus, is not something you can control. It is in God's gift alone. The Holy Spirit is like the wind, which '*blows wherever it pleases*' (John 3:8).

Of course, this produces objections such as, 'So I just have to wait for God, do I?' In fact, that is not the case. To be frank, you cannot even wait properly unless you are born again! No, Christ said this to Nicodemus, the proud Pharisee, in order to humble him, to remove his false confidence that he could save himself. Wherever people are sure of themselves and of their ability to please God and win their own salvation, the message of Jesus is: '"you must be born again"' by the Holy Spirit, and that is not in your hands.

However, if we are humbled, we may hear what Jesus went on to say to Nicodemus: '*God ... gave his one and only Son, that whoever believes in him shall not perish but have eternal life*' (John 3:16). Our responsibility is to repent and believe. God's work is to grant us the grace to do so. This is linked with the problem people find with God's sovereign choice of a people for himself. Do we have to wait and see if God has chosen us? No. Instead, we must obey the command of the gospel, 'Repent and believe' (Mark 1:15), and then we will know that we have been chosen, that God has given us the new birth, for without that we could never have turned to him at all.

This assertion of man's helplessness upsets many people, so they try to change the message. Free will and human ability replace God's power and grace, but the result is a different religion entirely. We cannot believe just what we choose to believe and still have the genuine article. And it is real, biblical Christianity, the gospel of grace and mercy through faith in Christ alone, that has changed men and women in the past and is still doing so. It is this alone that brings forgiveness and eternal life. Anything else is a human invention and cannot save anyone.

Facing the facts

By now, you may be wondering, 'Why are you insisting on all these objectionable things? It almost seems as if you are trying to put us off.' I have three reasons.

First, only the true gospel saves. It is God's salvation, and the ambassador of Christ has no authority to change the terms of his commission. What have I achieved if I gain thousands of adherents, but merely lead them astray? In any case, we should not judge a medicine by its taste but by its effectiveness. This is not to say, however, that something has to be unpleasant to work; indeed, the message of Jesus Christ is delightful good news, if we will only humble ourselves to receive it without quibbling at God's terms.

Secondly, it is essential that enquirers 'know the score', that they are aware beforehand of the demands and difficulties of the Christian life. Jesus himself followed this procedure. When certain men wanted to join the ranks of his disciples, he appeared to be doing his best to put them off. He warned them, *'Foxes have dens and birds have nests, but the Son of Man has nowhere to lay his head'* (Matthew 8:20). Was he trying to dissuade them? No, he wanted them to establish the cost correctly (Luke 14:28).

Finally, it is by considering these matters that people come to see themselves as they are. Then, by the working of the Holy Spirit, their objections are overcome. They realise the hardness of their own hearts, the blindness of their minds, the obstinacy of their wills. If he is working in you, then I have no fear that these necessary truths will put you off in the end. Instead, I believe that he will use them to draw you to Christ.

The important thing with genuine objections is to face up to them fairly and squarely, not to amend the gospel to fit popular opinion.

We cannot believe just what we like; we must accept what God has said. That is why I have tried to set out the real gospel in this chapter, and why the rest of this book, dealing with other objections, will use them to give a better understanding of the wonderful good news of Jesus Christ.

3.
'You can't prove it's true.'

Atheists and agnostics of every kind make this assertion above. Some have never thought seriously about the matter at all; it is just a convenient excuse. But there are others who are deadly serious, who base their lives and hopes on this denial. They realise that if Christianity should happen to be true, and they reject it, they will pay for their mistake with everything they are, for ever.

Again, others refuse to think precisely because they treat truth seriously. A Christian was once trying to talk to one such unbelieving young man. The young man refused to consider the subject at all. 'Come on,' said the Christian, 'you've got nothing to lose.' 'Oh yes I have,' was the answer; 'it might be true!' And if it were true he would have to change his whole lifestyle. This is sometimes why serious-minded people argue so vehemently: It is because they know that if they lose the argument, they must change their minds and convictions—and probably their lives as well. And that is too painful to do lightly. I assume that my readers take this attitude and I approve of it. This gives some point to the debate.

In many ways this is the most basic objection of all. For although there are some who would base their appeal on the fact that Christianity works (which it does) or on its long history (which it genuinely has) or on its intellectual satisfaction (which is real) we must, and do, take our stand on the fact that Christianity is true.

When Jesus was on trial before the Roman governor, Pontius Pilate, he claimed, '… *the reason I was born and came into the world is to testify to the truth*' (John 18:37). Pilate mockingly asked, *'What is truth?'* and left him. Possibly Pilate was the forerunner of many since then who say that everything is relative;

there are no absolutes. For this reason they do not care whether Christianity is true or not. However, this leaves them with no certainty, no sure foundation. It has been said that the only certain thing in life is death[6], but if everything is relative, then we have nothing to give hope or help when we most need it.

So this objection is most important. If this succeeds then the whole edifice of Christianity collapses. If it fails, then logically conversion must follow. So, can we prove that Christianity is true? In the first place, can we prove the existence of God? The answer is: 'We do not have to.'

God's existence

The apostles and others who preached the gospel in the New Testament never tried to prove that God existed. They simply assumed this. Sometimes, of course, they were speaking to Jews who they knew believed in the God of the Old Testament; that was enough. But even when they were speaking to Gentiles— heathen as we might call them today—they acted on the presupposition that everyone believes in at least the existence of God.

Even if the Gentiles were idol-worshippers, they spoke to them on the basis that those listening did really know the true God. Thus, we read how Paul and Barnabas at a place called Lystra addressed a crowd of people who worshipped the Greek gods; they included a priest of Zeus. The apostles did not confuse the true God with these '*worthless things*', but turned their hearers to '*the living God, who made the heavens and the earth and the sea and everything in them*' (Acts 14:15).

In Athens, the apostle Paul used the Greeks' altar '*TO AN UNKNOWN GOD*' (Acts 17:23) to talk to them about '*the God who made the world and everything in it*' (Acts 17:24). How could they do this? How can Christians speak meaningfully to those who call themselves atheists and agnostics today?

---

6   And even that is untrue if Jesus' return pre-empts death.

Paul gives the answer in his letter to the Christians at Rome. He reminds them that *'For since the creation of the world God's invisible qualities—his eternal power and divine nature—have been clearly seen, being understood from what has been made, so that people are without excuse'* (Romans 1:20). This does not merely mean that men ought to see God in creation; he describes them as actually knowing God (Romans 1:21), not in the full Christian sense of an established personal relationship, but sufficiently to be *'without excuse'* when they do not respond to him. Atheism is not an excuse; it is a confession of sin: *'For although they knew God, they neither glorified him as God nor gave thanks to him ... they did not think it worthwhile to retain the knowledge of God'* (Romans 1:21,28).

Everyone is aware of the existence of God. Later Paul explains that everyone has a conscience that bears witness to the realities of God's law, even Gentiles, who have never been taught the Ten Commandments (Romans 2:14-15). So, although people may call themselves atheists (and really mean it—I am not calling them liars or hypocrites!) this is only because they are suppressing the knowledge they have. And whenever their conscience pricks them or accuses someone else of doing 'wrong', it testifies that they really, in their heart of hearts, do believe in a final arbiter of right and wrong, in God himself. However hard you may try to suppress the knowledge of God, it is still there. God has not left himself without a foothold in your soul, and it is on this that the apostles relied when they preached.

The longer this suppression of God and the searing of the conscience go on, the harder it is to awaken it; the more difficult it is to remind people of what they know. However, we are not relying on human arguments or human skill. We go on with our witness, as at present, trusting God to bring this knowledge of himself into action once more. I cannot convince by arguments from the creation or from anything else; that has been done already. All that remains is for God to bring that belief back to the surface, and use it to convict the God-denier of his sin.

The next step for the objector is to dismiss Christianity because of the multiplicity of religions. 'How do you know yours is the true one? What about the Hindus, the Muslims, the Jehovah's Witnesses?', they ask. In answer, we must be clear that the knowledge we have been talking about is not merely belief in 'a god of some sort', 'someone or something out there', such as many admit to believing in. What creation reveals is the glory of God, the true God, the living God, the Maker of heaven and earth (Acts 14:15). This God, who has made himself known in creation —what is called 'general revelation'—has also made himself known in the Bible—'special revelation'. This is our authority for our beliefs and our gospel.

For our objector, of course, that merely moves the problem back one stage. 'How do you know your Bible is true?' is the next question. 'How do you prove that it is not just a collection of myths and legends?'

The Bible's authority

Again, the first answer—but not the whole answer—is that we do not have to. In fact one cannot in the nature of the case prove that something is the final authority, for that is what the Bible is. Whatever you appealed to for confirmation of the Bible's position would itself then become your final authority. That is, if scholars can prove that the Bible is the final authority then they are the final authority in fact—and so on and on. In practice many do treat the 'experts' like this, but as experts both change and contradict one another there is no future in it!

There used to be a philosophical school called 'Logical Positivism'. It has virtually vanished nowadays in its original form, but many people follow it without realising what they are doing. It taught that the only true knowledge is what you can prove by scientific observation. On these grounds, of course, religion of any kind must be rejected. And so it was until thinking men realised that the philosophers' assertion itself could not be proved by scientific observation! They were "hoist with their own petard".[7] Like us and everybody else, they were working from unprovable presuppositions.

So we do not prove the Bible; we preach it and it 'accredits itself'. It is self-authenticating. That is, God by the Holy Spirit convinces people that it is God's word and that it must be obeyed. As one preacher (C. H. Spurgeon) is supposed to have said, 'Defend the Bible? I would as soon defend a lion!'[8] What we do is set it free to defend itself when we use it to make known the gospel. This self-authentication is what I am relying on to convince the reader, not my arguments.

There is, however, more to be said. The Bible is the end result of a process of revelation by God, using his servants, such as the prophets and apostles, and especially his own Son, the Lord Jesus Christ. These messengers he accredited; he gave them credentials so that their hearers could know that they were sent by God. The Bible is, therefore, both the record of revelation and the revelation itself.

What sort of accreditation do men have? Leaving aside the prophets and apostles, who were often able to confirm their message with miracles, let us concentrate on Christ himself. There are two stages to his accreditation. First, as Acts 2:22 puts it, *'Jesus of Nazareth was a man accredited by God to you by miracles, wonders and signs, which God did among you through him, as you yourselves know.'* And they did know! Then, however, we come to the supreme confirmation of his authority— the resurrection from the dead.

The Jewish authorities had rejected him as a usurper and blasphemer. They denied his claims to be the Messiah and God's Son. He was a fraud, they said, and so they had him crucified. But when he rose from the dead all they could do was to hush it up, as the account of the bribing of the guards, recorded in

---

7   Hamlet Act 3, Scene 4. Etymology:
     https://en.wikipedia.org/wiki/Hoist_with_his_own_petard
8   C.H. Spurgeon, 1886 sermon *Christ and His Co-Workers*: "... stand back, and open the door, and let the lion out!"

Matthew (28:11-15), shows. So when Paul told the Athenians that God *'has set a day when he will judge the world with justice by the man he has appointed'*, he added the proof God had given, *'by raising him from the dead'* (Acts 17:31).

The story is told of a man who invented a new religion, but found that people were not interested. He consulted the ruler of his country and received the sound but shattering advice: 'Get yourself crucified and then rise from the dead and people will believe you.' When Christ rose he demonstrated beyond argument the truth of his teaching and especially of his claims.

The apostles were eyewitnesses of this and appealed to this fact when they preached: *'He was not seen by all the people, but by witnesses whom God had already chosen—by us who ate and drank with him after he rose from the dead. [42] He commanded us to preach to the people and to testify that he is the one whom God appointed as judge of the living and the dead.'* (Acts 10:41-42).

The writers of the Gospels, such as Luke, searched out such eyewitnesses and recorded their evidence (Luke 1:2). Thus we have in the Bible eyewitness evidence of the clearest kind from the finest men, evidence that should convince any unprejudiced reader. And these proofs were committed to writing at a time when they could have been refuted if untrue (2 Peter 1:16).

The apostle Paul claims 500 eyewitnesses of the resurrection in a letter written less than thirty years after the event (1 Corinthians 15:6). Surely some of them would have let the cat out of the bag if this had been an invention? Surely someone would have 'discovered' the occupied tomb or the decomposing body? It was certainly in the interests of many people to disprove the story if they could. But that is another subject.

The point is that the evidence for Christ's resurrection, even on ordinary human grounds, quite apart from the work of the Holy Spirit in producing the Bible as the infallible word of God, is seen to be utterly reliable. The apostles used their eyewitness evidence with great confidence in its validity, and we have that same evidence in written form today.

Please forget the silly stories that are circulated about the Bible's inaccuracy: "It was not written in the second century"; "it is just a collection of myths". The manuscript evidence is much better than for any other ancient document—and those are accepted without question[9]. Especially forget that silly story about oral transmission, which is supposed to discredit the New Testament record. This is the one about the general who passed an oral message, 'Send reinforcements; I'm going to advance,' which came out as 'Send three-and-fourpence; I'm going to a dance.' That story is just as out of date as the coinage! These authors were people living in a different era, when memory was not corrupted, or atrophied, by the convenient printed word and ubiquitous television.

All this I assert merely on the assumption of normal honesty, intelligence and memory. Most of the criticisms of the Bible seem to assume that the biblical writers were morons, madmen or confidence-tricksters, instead of the highly-skilled literary craftsmen that their writings show them to be. No other book and no other writers are treated in this way. I wonder why?

'Ah, yes,' says our objector, 'but how do you know you are right, and not the other people who appeal to the Bible?' This question is in many ways a non-starter, for most of those who take the Bible seriously as the infallible word of God agree on the basic gospel anyway. And this they have done down the centuries. This is most clearly seen since the Reformation of the sixteenth century. Since then there have always been Christians—many of them—who have believed what I am putting forward in this book.

While science, philosophy and unbiblical forms of 'Christianity' so-called have changed a dozen times or more, the evangelical message has remained unaltered. Why? Because it is based on the unchanging word of God. There are only two religious

---

9   For example, *Caesar's Gallic War* has two ancient manuscripts compared with over 5,000 for just the New Testament of the Bible.

systems which can have any claim to authenticity—Evangelical Protestantism and Roman Catholicism—and a simple examination will demonstrate that the first of these alone is consistent with the Bible.

This last handful of paragraphs has been included, not to prove the truth of the Bible or the rightness of our teaching. Their function is solely to remove the false ideas that are abroad and which may deceive the unwary. The best, perhaps the only, way to come to the truth of the matter is to follow the example of the apostles and their hearers. Paul and the rest appealed to the Bible as their authority and left their hearers to check it out. They proved from the Old Testament that Jesus was the promised Messiah and expected their hearers to put it to the test. Indeed, the Jews in Berea are commended as being *'of more noble character'* than others because they did just that. They *'examined the Scriptures every day to see if what Paul said was true'* (Acts 17:11). As a result, many of the Jews believed the gospel. The same result will follow if you honestly let the Bible speak for itself. You must, as I mentioned earlier, be a genuine seeker, prepared to act on what you find to be true. And if, unlike Pilate, you are prepared to consider the evidence fairly, you will be convinced.

4.
'I've got my own religion.'

This objection can be intended to end all discussion. It is often just a polite "brush-off", whether on the doorstep, or in the office, or wherever. The other 'religion' varies from Islam to Roman Catholicism. Whatever the nominal churchgoing claim, the objector does not want to be disturbed. It may even be a form of humanism, which the speaker regards as much better than any religion anyway!

I am not concerned, as I said earlier, with those who are merely avoiding the issue. I want to address those who sincerely feel that their present position is satisfactory, or that one should not change the religion in which one was reared. Many people have little inclination to practise their avowed religion, but adhere very closely to it if anyone suggests that they should change. There are countries where you cannot change your religion without dire consequences. In the West we may change, but most are not willing to do so.

Behind this attitude we sometimes find the opinion that all religions are really the same and that we might as well stick to the one we know. They all marry or bury you; they all want money from you. As long as you have a label to give the administrators if you go into hospital, it is all right. As an after-thought, we are often asked 'We all worship the same God anyway, don't we?'

As you will have gathered already, this is neither my opinion nor the teaching of the Bible. The word of God makes it abundantly clear that there are many false religions and only one true one (Acts 4:12). I am not going to argue for a mere change of church or denomination. That may be needed, but it cannot be the basic issue. The true religion is real Christianity in contrast with the many false versions as well as with non-Christian faiths.

There are many examples in the New Testament of people changing their 'religion', and I want to use one of these as a 'model' to illustrate this change and the reasons for it. The following extract is from Paul's first letter to the Thessalonians:

For we know, brothers and sisters loved by God, that he has chosen you, [5] because our gospel came to you not simply with words but also with power, with the Holy Spirit and deep conviction. You know how we lived among you for your sake. [6] You became imitators of us and of the Lord, for you welcomed the message in the midst of severe suffering with the joy given by the Holy Spirit. [7] And so you became a model to all the believers in Macedonia and Achaia. [8] The Lord's message rang out from you not only in Macedonia and Achaia—your faith in God has become known everywhere. Therefore, we do not need to say anything about it, [9] for they themselves report what kind of reception you gave us. They tell how you turned to God from idols to serve the living and true God, [10] and to wait for his Son from heaven, whom he raised from the dead – Jesus, who rescues us from the coming wrath. (1 Thessalonians 1:4-10)

The basic criterion for choosing a religion must always be the one discussed already: 'Is it true?' The Thessalonians chose *'the living and the true God'*. However, using their experience as a 'model', I want to ask four other questions of your present religion (or lack of one). Your answers may show why it is worthwhile investigating the truth of the Bible's claims.

Does your religion make sense of life?

Many people are puzzled and troubled by the injustices of life. Why is it that the wicked seem to get rich, that the criminals get away with it, in defiance of the old saying that cheats never prosper? Ordinary people easily become disillusioned when the millionaire raids the pension fund of the working man and nobody appears to notice or do anything about it. The writer of Psalm

73:3 tells how he *'saw the prosperity of the wicked'* and was puzzled by it. Job, similarly, asked,-

'Why do the wicked live on,
*   growing old and increasing in power? ...*

They spend their years in prosperity
*   and go down to the grave in peace.'* (Job 21:7,13)

The question is often raised in the Bible and everywhere the same answer is given: that a day is coming when God will judge men and punish evildoers. This is true of the 1 Thessalonians 1:10, quoted above; Paul says that they are waiting for the return of the Lord Jesus Christ, a day of *'coming wrath'*. The one who came the first time as a Saviour will come again as Judge.

His judgement will be true and just (Romans 2:2); he will not judge by mere appearances, but according to his perfect knowledge (Isaiah 11:3b-4b). There will be no miscarriages of justice then, no fabricating of the evidence, no false confessions or perjured statements. Everybody will receive exactly what he deserves, as we read in Christ's own words: *'For the Son of Man is going to come in his Father's glory with his angels, and then he will reward each person according to what they have done.'* (Matthew 16:27) Christ will come again, and all wrongs will be put right, all injustices corrected. All will make sense at last. What many forget, however, is that this judgement will include not only the Hitlers, Stalins and Putins of this world but everybody, including themselves. And no one is without sin. This, therefore, makes our next criterion of great importance.

Does your religion give you a clear conscience?

We are told that many of the people being treated in psychiatric hospitals would not need to be there if their sense of guilt could only be dealt with. Some will have a genuine guilt 'complex'; they are anxious wrongly and unnecessarily; they have an obsession with some fault, imagined or exaggerated, which cannot be treated using only logic or common sense. They are mentally ill. These too may receive help from the gospel of Christ, but it is not with them that I am concerned at this point.

The people I am thinking of are those who often have a sincere belief in God, an acceptance of the Ten Commandments (Exodus 34:28; 20:1-17) and an awareness that they do not and cannot measure up to God's standards and requirements. In other words, they are bothered about real sin and real guilt, not just guilty feelings which have no basis in reality. I suspect that there are more of these people than we might imagine, but they hide their worry under a mask of indifference. They want peace of conscience and may think that they have found it, until they think about dying or their conscience is awakened by some new sin or a reminder of an old one.

Of the various devices adopted to gain some sort of peace, the most common is to convince ourselves that as long as we do our best everything will be 'all right in the end'. Sincerity, not perfection, is all that is required, and so we hope to achieve that. The trouble with this theory is twofold: the word of God does not support it and, when the crunch comes, experience is not satisfied with it. This may be the case even with those who maintain that there is no judgement and no hell. When they face death they will wish they had had a more secure foundation for their sense of peace.

This is particularly true of those who have committed some 'terrible' sin, in their youth or even later, which makes them feel defiled. At times, they can suppress their guilt, but then something awakens it, and they are in great distress. Their religion does not help; it only aggravates the situation, for they have nothing to rely on except themselves and, if they are defiled in their own eyes, how much more in God's!

Others adopt the way of works-salvation—trying to earn their acceptance with God by good deeds of various kinds. Some put their stress on religious deeds and church rituals. They are the heirs of several groups in the Bible: the Old Testament Jews who turned the law of Moses into a way of salvation and thought they could be worthy of the kingdom of God, and the Pharisees in Christ's day who claimed to be 'faultless' in terms of obeying the law. They thought that the works of religion—circumcision, ceremonies, sacrifices—could earn God's approval.

Their modern counterparts speak rather of baptism, confirmation, church-membership, giving their collection money, etc., but the end is the same—a belief that they have earned the favour of God. On the scales of God's justice, their good works outweigh the bad works, the religious zeal more than balances the sin. But as Paul pointed out to the Galatians, anyone adopting this approach *'is required to obey the whole law'* (Galatians 5:3). Part will not do. In the words of James, *'Whoever keeps the whole law and yet stumbles at just one point is guilty of breaking all of it'* (James 2:10). The law is like a chain: break one link and the whole chain is broken. *'If you do not commit adultery … but do commit murder, you have become a law-breaker.'* (James 2:11) The one sin—and we all have committed many more than one— is sufficient proof that the man or woman is sinful and that the whole life is defiled. We are all rebels against God and nothing from such a source is acceptable. It is like someone getting in the washing from the line with dirty hands; every garment bears the filthy marks.

Others, especially today, claim that the works necessary are those of charity: helping the needy, the hungry, the ill, the poor of this world. They may quote the words of Christ in support of this position. In Matthew 25 we have the account of the Day of Judgement when Christ, the King, will assess people on the basis of their treatment of 'the least of these brothers of mine' (Matthew 25:40). These brothers are quite wrongly identified by some as being anyone in need, so that anyone who helps them is said to have done it to Christ. In fact, these brothers are Christ's disciples, so that the good deeds are done for them because they are Christ's disciples and thus out of love for Christ.

Such works do not earn salvation; they merely demonstrate that the doer is one of Christ's people. This does not, of course, rule out helping any needy people as an act of Christian compassion and concern, but that is not a proof of loving Christ. All sorts of people do this kind of 'good deed', but it does not make them Christ's, or reconcile them to God. This we cannot do by ourselves. The same problem remains. Enemies in time of war may do a lot of good to their fellow-countrymen by human standards, but they remain enemies. So it is with rebels against God.

Other forms of religion are followed in an attempt to find peace of mind and conscience, but without success. Some make much of confessing their sins to a priest, but the very fact that this has to be repeated time and time again shows that it is ineffective, even apart from being unscriptural. Others go to mass every day but, like one lady I met, have no hope beyond death except of going to purgatory.[10] Again, even apart from the fact that the Bible knows nothing of a third destiny beside heaven and hell, this shows how unavailing and unsatisfactory these remedies are—all that effort, and then only punishment in purgatory to look forward to! The best and most diligent Jehovah's Witness, with all her witnessing and door-knocking, can have no assurance about surviving '*Armageddon*' (Revelation 16:16) since it all depends on her.

Thankfully the Bible speaks of something far better: a salvation that does not depend on us, which provides forgiveness and cleansing and peace of conscience. Our 'control' passage in 1 Thessalonians speaks of this. These men had been heathen, living in bondage to idols and, apparently, fearful of the judgement. How much they must have rejoiced to be told of a Saviour, '*Jesus, who rescues us from the coming wrath*' (1 Thessalonians 1:10). The gospel tells of how '*Christ Jesus came into the world to save sinners*' (1 Timothy 1:15). Jesus Christ

---

10   In Roman Catholic doctrine, a place or state of suffering inhabited by the souls of sinners who are paying for their sins before going to heaven.

does not merely give us a helping hand or strengthen us to save ourselves. He does not just teach or give an example; he saves.

Put at its simplest, Jesus removed God's wrath from his people by dying to take it in their place. So, when the true Christian considers his sin, he does not deny it or minimise it. He simply says, 'Christ bore the punishment in my place, and now I am free. My conscience is clear.' He does not 'hope' in the vague modern sense that he may be all right in the end. He knows that his sin has been dealt with fully and finally. Does your religion, of whatever kind it may be, give you this peace and certainty when you think of dying and facing God?

Does it guarantee you eternal life?

Put another way this question asks, 'Does your religion deal with death? Does it give a sure and certain hope, not by denying sin but by removing it?' There is much fear of death about in this country. The reason some subjects, for example—cancer, are taboo is that men and women are afraid of dying. Roundabout expressions like 'passing away' are commonplace in conversations which show this fear.

This, of course, is nothing new. The people of New Testament times lived in fear and hopelessness. The so-called 'mystery religions'[11] were one way of trying to deal with this problem, but without success. One reason why the gospel spread so rapidly was that it answered man's deepest need at this point. The word 'hope' occurs many times in the New Testament and this shows just how relevant it was—and still is.

Other religions attempt to 'cash in' on this need, but the Christian message is unique in that it does not give easy consolation without dealing with sin. Spiritualism appeals to many who have lost a loved one by offering to put them in touch with those who have 'passed over', but this is a fraud, however well-intentioned some practitioners may be. It completely ignores the real basis of

---

11   A religion based on secret or mystical rites for initiates, especially in a number of cults popular during the late Roman Empire.

fear—the awareness of sin and the coming judgement. It assumes that all is well for everybody, that there is a pleasant home for everyone in the great beyond, irrespective of how they have lived and died. What comfort is it really to be assured that your loved ones are happy, if the same applies to Hitler and his friends? What kind of 'heaven' is that? It has to be admitted, of course, that there are some versions of Christianity—utterly false ones—that say the same. Too many funerals of unbelievers are designed to give comfort and peace where there should be none. The Bible does not teach a universal salvation.

Others, especially those influenced by Eastern religions or the New Age movement, believe in reincarnation. This must not be confused, as it often is, with the Bible's teaching about being born again (regeneration), which is a spiritual change that happens by the power of the Holy Spirit in this life. Reincarnation is the idea that after death we will return to this world in a different form, usually higher or lower, depending on how we have lived in this life. Much stress is laid on 'anecdotal evidence', i.e., people who claim to remember a previous existence or to have knowledge which demands such a hypothesis. One consequence of this belief is the convenient removal of responsibility for sin, since my present condition is the result of a previous existence and not 'my' fault at all.

Against all these ideas, the Bible teaches clearly that *'people are destined to die once, and after that to face judgement'* (Hebrews 9:27). But it does not stop there; it goes on to affirm that Christ won eternal life for his people. Those who believe in him have *'this hope as an anchor for the soul, firm and secure'* (Hebrews 6:19). It may be necessary to point out that *'hope'* as used in the Bible is not the vague optimism reflected, for instance, in the words: 'I hope it will be fine tomorrow.' That just means it might happen and I would like it to happen. The Bible's hope is of something still in the future, but promised by God and therefore certain.

The basis for this is in the resurrection of Christ. In our passage we read of Christians waiting for *'his Son from heaven, whom he raised from the dead'*. This confirms that death has been defeated once and for all. So those who are Christians know that death has lost its sting—there is no condemnation and punishment to follow—and death has lost its power—one day our bodies will be raised to share in eternal life with our souls. Meanwhile the Christian departs to *'be with Christ, which is better by far'* (Philippians 1:23). Does your religion give this kind of hope? If not, then it is not of much use.

Has it changed your life?

It is essential to include this subject, as otherwise we lay ourselves open to the charge of simply telling people what they want to hear. There are many whose religion is just wishful thinking; they take the comfort and ignore the demands. They go to church on Sunday and like to think that all will be well with their souls, but their life is not really affected. This may appear adequate for a time, but in the end it will be found to be a delusion. The reality is far from that; the Christian message, as I have already made clear, demands genuine repentance of those who want to enjoy its benefits.

However, it is also possible, and indeed necessary, to see this topic as one of those benefits. There are some who want their lives to be changed. They are those who have fallen so deeply into sin that they have become fed up with it. This may be just one particular sin, by which they are enslaved, or the life of sin as a whole, of which they have become tired because they have found that *'The way of transgressors is hard'* (Proverbs 13:15 AV, Authorized Version). Such people begin to seek something, often not even knowing what they want. It may be that they meet a real Christian and realise, as so many have testified, 'He had something I hadn't got, and that I wanted for myself.'

Paul's readers in Thessalonica were Christians like that. When the apostle reached Achaia, expecting to preach the gospel there, he found that he did not *'need to say anything about it'* (1 Thessalonians 1:8); they had already heard of the great change in the Thessalonians. They could tell him how the Thessalonians had *'turned to God from idols to serve the living and true God'* (1 Thessalonians 1:9). For some this change is sudden and very obvious to others; for others, perhaps because they have lived broadly moral and churchgoing lives, the change is less clear—at least at first. However, the same applies to all in the end. According to his own words, Christ came that we *'may have life, and have it to the full'* (John 10:10).

When people believe in Christ, when they are born again, their lives are transformed. How could it be otherwise? The terms that are used in the New Testament to describe conversion, such as the new birth, spiritual resurrection and new creation, must imply a great change. This is new life; the power of the Holy Spirit is made effective in them. There must be a change.

This is the glory of the Christian message. God does not merely forgive and forget. If he did no more than that, then sin would not really be dealt with. The glory of the gospel is that God speaks to the helpless and gives them new life. He does not wait for them to lift themselves out of the moral mud and mire before he will accept them. There would not be many Christians if that were the case! No, he rescues sinners from their sin and misery.

The story has often been told of the three religious teachers in India, looking at a drunk lying in the gutter. The Christian asked the others what they had to offer the man. The Hindu said that if the man lived a good life he could promise him a better future in his next incarnation. The Muslim said that if the man would only follow the rules of Islam—pray, give alms and even go on a pilgrimage to Mecca—then he could be sure of heaven. The drunk's response was predictable. How could he do anything to get himself out of the gutter? Only the Christian could say, 'My Saviour came to seek and to save that which was lost (Luke 19:10). He offers salvation from both the guilt and the power of sin, as a free gift.'

Only Christianity begins where people are, and saves them. Every other religion depends on people own power and ability to lift themselves by their own bootstraps. God, we are told, helps those who help themselves; but if you cannot do that, too bad! The helpless sinner is left in his lost and helpless condition. Do not mistake what I am saying. I am not referring only to down-and-outs. Everyone is like that; it is just that some are more obviously helpless than others. All need to be saved; you need to be saved. No one can save himself, but the gospel, as Paul tells the Romans, is the power of God for the salvation of everyone who believes (Romans 1:16).

These are the criteria for a worthwhile religion (remember we have already dealt with the issue of truth). Only a religion which fulfils all these needs can truly be called a gospel—good news. And only real Christianity fits the bill.

5.
'You don't have to go to church to be a Christian.'

Like many of the other objections made to becoming a Christian, this one has more than a grain of truth in it. It springs, at least in part, from the popular misconception that going to church does make you a Christian. That is no more true than the notion that living in a garage makes you a motor-car, but even so it is true that you cannot dissociate Christianity from church-going.

There are many who attend a place of worship, whose lives are no better, and are sometimes much worse, than the lives of those who spend their Sundays at the seaside. Of these some will probably be 'seekers', that is, they are still enquiring and have not committed themselves to being members of the church and living according to its standards. But, even if we rule out the 'churches' which are not real churches, i.e., where the true gospel is not taught and the members do not even claim to be saved or born again, we are still left with some who 'let the side down', who are real hypocrites. Nevertheless, the fact that we can recognise hypocrites, like the existence of forged ten-pound notes, implies that the genuine article also exists. All we need are the proper criteria for distinguishing the true from the false, and these we will try to provide.

The element of truth in the objection does not lie in the existence of hypocrites, but in the undoubted fact that you do not have to go to church to pray; you do not have to attend a church service to meet with God. No one claims that those who are house-bound or too isolated from other Christians are excluded from the number of God's people. This, however, begs the question: 'Is there, in fact, good reason for attending church?' In my view there are two good reasons for so doing.

The first is because you are a Christian and taking part in the life of the church is the proper and, in normal circumstances, the necessary response to God's mercy. This provides an opportunity for finding help in living the Christian life as well as for serving God together with other Christians. 'No man is an island'[12], the Christian least of all. Christ has established his church for these functions and Christian obedience will find it necessary to be part of the church. In this sense, you do have to go to church if you are a Christian.

The second reason for attending is to find out how to become a Christian. This involves no commitment to the church, no implication that you have believed already—so no hypocrisy is involved—and this is the way that many have come to faith in the Lord Jesus Christ. For others, however, it may not be the best way; they prefer to consider the issues privately, before taking, what is to them, a rather serious, and often difficult, step by actually going into a church building. I can sympathise with this and feel that many churches need to take this problem seriously. We must go out to meet the enquirer, not expect him to come to us, although we should continue to welcome those, perhaps with a religious background, who do adopt that approach. This book is an attempt to meet non-Christians on their own ground.

The only real answer to this objection, which avoids all these qualifications and maybes is to ask, 'What is a Christian?' Then the link with churchgoing will become abundantly clear. The Bible is the obvious place to look for a definition. True, words can change their meaning, but when there are those who still use the biblical meaning it is sensible to go back to the original use. We can actually do better than that and go back to the first ever use of the word, in the Acts of the Apostles. There we are told, in Acts 11:26, *'The disciples were called Christians first at Antioch.'*

---

12   John Donne, *Meditation 17*, 1623.

The basic meaning of the word seems to be "Christ-ones', a nickname given to them by the unbelieving inhabitants around them, but which they clearly adopted with pride. It must have been obvious from their words that this 'Christ', the Messiah, meant everything to them and this is the prime characteristic of a Christian. He is Christ's man; he will speak of Christ, show his respect and love for Christ in such a way that the people around will know that he is a Christian. How strange it is that we can meet those who claim to be Christians, and who are most upset if they think you are doubting this—after all, they go to church(!)—but who never use the name of Christ, never speak of him with love and devotion. If the name depended today on that kind of evidence, their neighbours would certainly not use this nickname about them. What then is a Christ-one?

A believer in Christ

Verses 19 to 30 of this chapter, Acts 11, describe the foundation of the church in Antioch. Some disciples, who had been driven out of Jerusalem by persecution, arrived in the city and began to preach the gospel to the Jews and then to the Gentile inhabitants. We are told that *'a great number of people believed'* their message (Acts 11:21). The content of this preaching is clear: *'the good news about the Lord Jesus'* (v.20). The rest of Acts and, indeed, of the New Testament, tells us that this *'good news'* involved Christ's coming into the world as the Saviour from sin, his death on the cross in the place of sinners, and his readiness to receive and forgive all who put their trust in him.

The Jews had been expected to recognise him as the promised Saviour, their Messiah, and find in him the salvation—forgiveness, eternal life, etc.—which they could not find in trying, vainly, to keep the law of Moses (Acts 13:38-39). The non-Jews made a marvellous discovery—that instead of slavery to their old gods (idols) they could find redemption from sin and the gift of eternal life, again by faith in Jesus Christ, God's Son.

Christians, then, are believers in Christ. This believing, we must be clear, is not just assenting to certain facts about Jesus, although that is included. Christian faith does not stop at believing that he existed, that he died on the cross, even that he rose again from the dead. It involves not just the mind but the heart, not just believing 'that' anything, but believing in or upon, that is, personal trust in, and commitment to, this Saviour. The individual hands over his eternal destiny to Christ and trusts him to rescue him from hell and grant salvation in all its fulness.

This is an inward and spiritual matter, far removed from mere church attendance, far more than attempts to keep the Ten Commandments or conform to the rules of the church. There is, however, an outward element; they must have confessed their faith publicly. Otherwise, of course, their neighbours would have known nothing about this so as to call them 'Christians', those who believe in Christ. People we meet today who insist that their faith is a private matter, thus attempting to get rid of a persistent Christian worker, thereby demonstrate that they are not Christians. Real faith not only believes in the heart; it also confesses with the mouth (Romans 10:10). Real Christians want to talk about the Lord who loved them and gave himself for them. Thus they show, and others know, that they are Christ-ones.

A disciple of Christ

Faith in Christ is always accompanied by conversion, or turning to Christ. So we are told, in the account of the church at Antioch, that they *'believed and turned to the Lord'* (Acts 11:21). Conversion is a term we are used to in many connections; people are converted to or from Roman Catholicism, to or from communism or vegetarianism. In every case (apart from the mechanical ones like being converted to North Sea gas![13]) there is the idea of a new loyalty, a new allegiance, be it to a person or a cause or a principle. A change of belief leads to a change of behaviour and lifestyle. This is the case pre-eminently with

---

13   This happened in the UK from approximately 1967 to 1977.

Christian conversion. These new believers were now Christ's people; they belonged to him; they were at his disposal.

So when Barnabas arrived from Jerusalem to help the infant church, he *'saw what the grace of God had done'*, as the inhabitants of Antioch had already seen. The first thing he did, when he realised that this was a genuine work of God, was to encourage *'them all to remain true to the Lord with all their hearts'* (Acts 11:23).

It was this allegiance to King Jesus that sent many first-century Christians to their death; since Christ possessed them, body and soul, there was no way they could take an absolute oath of allegiance to Caesar. That would have involved not simply submitting to the powers that be, as the apostles had commanded, but recognising the emperor as an absolute monarch and even as a god himself. The same has been true of many later generations, whether in Western Europe during the Reformation struggle or in twentieth-century Eastern Europe. No wonder the people in Antioch called them Christ-ones; he was their Lord and Master; they would obey him come what may.

Christians, then, are disciples, followers, not mere fans. Their attitudes and wills have been changed. They lead a new life of obedience to their King. They are consecrated to his service. Their loyalty is to him, not in the first place to a church. Any amount of churchgoing will not accomplish this kind of change; only the power of the Holy Spirit can do that. Conversion is God's work, enabling people to turn to the Lord. Their loyalty to the church comes only as an expression of that prior loyalty, for it is his church; he is the head and they are members of his body.

It is, therefore, quite wrong to think that the church does not matter. Going to church does not make you a disciple, but disciples of Christ already belong to the church of which their Master is head. Disciples of Christ will obey him for he has instituted the church for their benefit.

Even in the Gospel of Matthew we find Christ assuming that his church will be established and continue; he gives instructions for its discipline and life (Matthew 16:18; 18:15-20). We may conclude, then, that you do not have to go to church to become a Christian, but if you become one, you also become a disciple and serve your Lord in his church. In the following verses this is what we see the new believers at Antioch doing.

Added to Christ

Through the ministry of Barnabas many, we read, *'were brought to the Lord'* (Acts 11:24). Literally this is 'were added to the Lord'. This expression also occurs in chapter 2, where we find twice that new believers were *'added to their number'* (Acts 2:41,47). Together these references and the description in chapter 11 make it clear that to be added to Christ was to be added also to the church; you could not have one without the other. So we read that when Barnabas brought Saul (better known as Paul) to share the work with him, they *'met with the church and taught great numbers of people'* (Acts 11:26). The word *'with'* tells us that for them Christianity is not so much going to church as being the church.

Thus, apart from the obvious exceptions already noted, you cannot be a Christian without being part of the visible church. If you are added to Christ, you are added to his church; if you are not added to his church then you have not been 'added to' Christ and, therefore, you have not been saved. It is important at this point to remember that we are not here adopting an exclusive attitude which says, 'You must belong to my church or you are not saved.' The old Roman Catholic principle was: 'Outside the church no salvation,' and they meant the Roman Catholic church! And others have followed them. It must, of course, be a real biblical church, but not necessarily of one particular denominational label. We are talking about the church, the body of Christ. Nevertheless, this must be represented by particular local congregations; the New Testament makes it very clear that you can only belong to the universal church by being part of a local church.

Furthermore, belonging is not just having your name on a membership list. Vast numbers of British people deceive themselves with that. They claim to be 'C of E' (or Methodist or Baptist or whatever), perhaps when going into hospital or wanting to arrange a funeral, but this says nothing at all about their actual beliefs or commitment. Belonging to Christ's church means not only having experienced a Christian conversion, but also sharing in the spiritual life (not just the jumble sales!) of a church with others who have had that same experience.

When Paul and Barnabas assembled with the church at Antioch, it was for a specific purpose, that of teaching the believers. It was these people, meeting for instruction, who were recognised and called Christians (Acts 11:26). Sadly, there are many who have made some kind of open profession of faith, perhaps at a large meeting or rally, who do not attach themselves to a church. They neither want nor receive teaching, support or encouragement, and their apparent 'faith' withers and dies. More must be said about this in a later chapter, but for the moment we must note that Christ's intention for his people is that they worship, work and witness together as his people, his church. There is a real sense in which we can define being a Christian, as distinct from becoming a Christian, as one who is part of a true church and who, in the words of Acts 2:42, devotes himself *'to the apostles' teaching and to fellowship, to the breaking of bread and to prayer'.*

Christians are believers, disciples and brothers. They are added to the number of Christ's family and their whole life shows this. They cannot just stay at home; they want to learn more. They cannot just watch television; they want to join in worship. They cannot just keep quiet; they want to share with others the good news about salvation that they have discovered. We must not sideline the church, merely because there are so many who do not in any way measure up to biblical criteria. If the truth is preached, if Christian living is encouraged, if love is fostered, if the message of God's grace is spread, then a real Christian will play his or her part.

In the end it is not a matter of whether a Christian must go to church. He or she will want to do so; the church will be his life. Instead of the brinkmanship which says, 'How little can I do and still count myself a Christian?' he will be doing as much as he can to serve and glorify the Christ who has died to save him.

6.
'I can't believe in a God of love.'

I want to deal with this objection in a rather different way from those we have considered so far. When I am faced by someone who challenges the love of God in this way I want to reply like the Irishman who was asked the way to Dublin. He answered, 'Sure and if was going to Dublin I wouldn't start from here.' Similarly I want to start, not from the objection, but from the Bible's actual teaching about the love of God. The reason for this is that the subject is so confused in the minds of many people. It is a very emotive topic and too many get so worked up that they do not, and cannot, listen properly or think clearly.

For instance, there are many who do believe in a God of love, but it is not the love that the Bible describes. Because of this they assume that all is well with them and their religion, while all the time they are rejecting the gospel.

However, the position which the chapter heading really represents is that which looks at all the disasters in the world, or more narrowly in their own life, and says, 'In the light of all this I cannot believe in this loving God you tell me about.' But people who say this may not really have been told accurately. It may be a counterfeit note that they are rejecting, while the genuine one is out of their sight.

In other words, I hope to kill two birds with one stone. In both cases the root of the trouble is a false idea, a wrong preconception of what God's love is like, or ought to be like. Both groups of people have begun from their own man-made definition of what they think God ought to do and assume that this is what the Christian message teaches. The safe way, and I hope the most helpful way, is to start from the Bible's teaching about God's love—in other words, from what God has himself revealed about his love. At least in this way we should know what we are supposed to be arguing about!

God is love

The apostle John, in his first letter, has a passage which concentrates on this very topic and so this is a suitable place for us to begin:

Dear friends, let us love one another, for love comes from God. Everyone who loves has been born of God and knows God. [8] Whoever does not love does not know God, because God is love. [9] This is how God showed his love among us: he sent his one and only Son into the world that we might live through him. [10] This is love: not that we loved God, but that he loved us and sent his Son as an atoning sacrifice for our sins. [11] Dear friends, since God so loved us, we also ought to love one another. [12] No one has ever seen God; but if we love one another, God lives in us and his love is made complete in us.

[13] This is how we know that we live in him and he in us: he has given us of his Spirit. [14] And we have seen and testify that the Father has sent his Son to be the Saviour of the world. [15] If anyone acknowledges that Jesus is the Son of God, God lives in them and they in God. [16] And so we know and rely on the love God has for us. God is love ... (1 John 4:7-16)

You will have noticed that John does not write merely about God's love; he goes much further: '*God*', he says (twice), '*is love.*' We are not considering just one attribute of God; his essential being is love. This is true also of his powerful, divine nature, referred to as '*spirit*'—'*God is spirit*' (John 4:24)—and his holiness—'*God is light*' (1 John 1:5). It is impossible for God to deny these aspects of his being in practice. His love is a holy love and his holiness is loving holiness. It is impossible to understand this fully, but it should make us wary, to say the least, of jumping to conclusions about God when we come across difficulties in our knowledge or experience.

Universal love

One facet of the Bible's teaching tells us that God loves everything that he has made. This includes the world itself, the creatures he has made in the world and all mankind simply as his creation. Some verses speak of his kindness, his compassion and his mercy, but even the word *'love'* is used:

[speaking of *the LORD*]
'who by his understanding made the heavens;
  his love endures for ever.' (Psalm 136:5).

For this reason he gives good gifts to mankind, even though they have become his enemies. Thus, in the Sermon on the Mount, Jesus urges his disciples to love their enemies and pray for those who persecute them, on the ground that this is the pattern set by their heavenly Father, who *'causes his sun to rise on the evil and the good, and sends rain on the righteous and the unrighteous'* (Matthew 5:44-45).

Far from complaining, then, we ought to be grateful for the gifts we receive. We deserve only his anger, because of our sin, but God gives good and perfect gifts (James 1:17). This is not just a sort of tolerance, a sop to keep the masses quiet. According to Paul's sermon to the idol-worshippers at Lystra, God has a more merciful aim in all this. *'Yet he has not left himself without testimony: He has shown kindness by giving you rain from heaven and crops in their seasons; he provides you with plenty of food and fills your hearts with joy'* (Acts 14:17). In his letter to the Romans this same apostle asks whether they are showing *'contempt for the riches of* [God's] *kindness, forbearance and patience, not realising that God's kindness is intended to lead you to repentance ...'* (Romans 2:4).

Already, then, we have good reason to doubt our doubts about God's love. If he loves even enemies like this and gives them gifts instead of pouring out wrath on them, then it is most unlikely that he is unloving in his dealings with us in other cases. Surely we must have misunderstood. A child who is used to experiencing nothing but kindness from her father will at least give him the benefit of the doubt when something untoward happens. Furthermore, if God assures us that he wants us to come back to him and confirms this by his kindness and loving gifts, we should hesitate to deduce the opposite when things appear to contradict this.

The fact is, we deserve nothing from the hand of God but anger and punishment for our sins, and to receive anything good from him is a matter of grace and mercy—a bonus, not a shortfall. In any case, we could not complain if God simply refused to have anything more to do with us, if he banished us instantly from his presence. Even his judgements are intended as warnings at this stage of history. The sad thing is, as we are reminded in the last book of the Bible, that when God's warning judgements have come on people, *'they cursed the name of God, who had control over these plagues, but they refused to repent and glorify him.'* (Revelation 16:9).

Provision of a Saviour

The passage I quoted from John's first letter does not refer to God's universal love; instead, it goes much further. John is concerned, not with mere temporal gifts, but with the gift of God's own Son to be a Saviour. Sadly this is ignored by most who complain about a perceived lack of love in God. They think only of matters connected with happiness and pain—the material and the physical. But even if there were no gifts of food and pleasure, no expressions of kindness and mercy in God's providence, this one gift would be sufficient to declare God to be '*love*' indeed. *'This is how God showed his love among us: He sent his one and only Son into the world that we might live through him.'* (1 John 4:9) This love did not stop at sending him into this world, great as that would have been. God sent him to die on the cross as *'an atoning sacrifice'* (1 John 4:10), to bear the punishment of sinners so that God might forgive them and save them.

Paul makes the same point, perhaps even more strongly, in Romans 5:8: *'God demonstrates his own love for us in this: While we were still sinners, Christ died for us.'* He also uses the terms *'powerless'*, *'ungodly'* and *'God's enemies'* to make clear just how great this *'love'* is. God did not give his Son for nice, righteous people; he did not give him as a reward for our making the first step or approach. No, says John, *'This is love: not that we loved God, but that he loved us and sent his Son as an atoning sacrifice for our sins.'* (1 John 4:10)

It is important to realise at this point that God's love does not ignore sin, as many think today; that is the dangerous misconception to which I referred earlier. He is holy and just, and neither will nor can simply take no notice when his creatures sin. What he did do is far more wonderful: He dealt with that sin by making his own Son an atoning sacrifice or propitiation, bearing the punishment on the cross so that God's just wrath and anger might be turned away from those who truly deserved it.

When that greatest of all 'love texts', John 3:16, tells us that *'God so loved the world that he gave his one and only Son,'* it is not only the breadth of the love that is in view but also, and especially, its depth, for the term *'world'* indicates a people and a system in settled opposition to the living God. For such people such a Son was given. The story of Abraham and Isaac gives a pale foreshadowing of this amazing love. In fact, the New Testament wording appears deliberately to recall that event. When God tested Abraham's faithfulness to him, he told him, *'Take your son, your only son, Isaac, whom you love, and go to the region of Moriah. Sacrifice him there as a burnt offering'* (Genesis 22:2). God stressed the relationship of love so that the sacrifice would appear in its true colours. So it is with God's love; his love for his one and only Son makes his willingness to sacrifice him out of love for lost mankind appear all the greater.

The offer of mercy

Although Christ died in a specific sense only for the people whom God had given to him before the foundation of the world, the elect, there is another sense in which this love of God applies to all. Although Christ does not save all, he is a Saviour for all who will put their trust in him. In the gospel he is set before all as Saviour. In this sense John and, before him, the Samaritan woman in John 4:42 use the term *'the Saviour of the world'*. John puts it in another way in 1 John 5:11-12: *'And this is the testimony: God has given us eternal life, and this life is in his Son. *12* Whoever has the Son has life; whoever does not have the Son of God does not have life.'* He has not given this life to all absolutely, but this love of God, wide beyond all our imagining, has provided a Saviour whom he offers freely to all, and with him eternal life.

God '[takes] *no pleasure in the death of the wicked, but rather that they turn from their ways and live'* (Ezekiel 33:11). He even pleads with people to be reconciled. The task of the preacher is to plead on God's behalf: *'... And he has committed to us the message of reconciliation. *20* We are therefore Christ's ambassadors, as though God were making his appeal through us. We implore you on Christ's behalf: be reconciled to God.'* (2 Corinthians 5:19-20). This is love indeed. If God has loved you like this, can you complain? It is God who has real cause for complaint. Like Ezekiel's countrymen of old, you are saying, *'The way of the Lord is not just'* (Ezekiel 33:17), to which he can reply, 'It is your way that is not just. You reject the love I offer, despise the salvation I plead with you to accept, and then complain that I do not love you!'

If God has loved me to this extent then I must be prepared to trust him for all the rest of his dealings with me. If he has made such a sacrifice, then it cannot be a lack of love that lies behind them. Perhaps the trouble is that you have never before heard properly about the love of God. You have not seen its greatness and undeservedness, and so have the wrong perspective on life in general. The proper way is to view everything through the spectacles provided by God's real love as seen in the giving of Christ. These are not falsely rose-tinted, but clear and true. And even this is not the full story of God's love. For the Christian there is much more.

God's special love

The deepest kind of love which God displays is his electing and redeeming love. Even before creation God loved his chosen or elected ones. He gave them to his Son, whom he sent into the world specifically to save them—not just to make it possible, not merely to offer it, but actually to save. This is love indeed! According to the apostle Paul, *'He chose us in* [Christ] *before the creation of the world to be holy and blameless in his sight. In love* [5] *he predestined us for adoption to sonship through Jesus Christ, in accordance with his pleasure and will ...'* (Ephesians 1:4-5).

We have already seen the reference to this love in Romans 5—a love for enemies, ungodly rebels, which assures us that this love is gracious love, free and undeserved, the gift of God's sovereign, unmerited grace. This is a love, therefore, which nothing can remove or destroy. Since I did not deserve it in the past, I cannot forfeit it by lack of deserving in the present. In his love God forbears with me and shows long-suffering towards me. This does not, of course, mean that I can live and do as I like, for his love has also changed me inwardly. That is a separate objection, to which we will return. Suffice it for now to remember that, according to Ephesians 1:4, God's electing love is an election *'to be holy'*, so I cannot presume upon it. If am not becoming holy, then I have no right to claim to be one of his chosen.

This, then, is a love that continues to the end. In Romans 8:32, Paul deduces from God's loving gift of his Son that all else that we need for our final salvation will be given to us too. The greater —greatest—gift guarantees the lesser: *'He who did not spare his own Son, but gave him up for us all—how will he not also, along with him, graciously give us all things?'* Those who doubt the love of God should read on to the end of the chapter as Paul waxes lyrical (but it is literally true) about the love of God. *'Who shall separate us from the love of Christ?'* (Romans 8:35), he asks. The answer is, 'Nothing and nobody, not even death.' In everything, he continues, *'we are more than conquerors through him who loved us.'* (Romans 8:37) There is nothing, he concludes, that *'will be able to separate us from the love of God that is in Christ Jesus'* (Romans 8:39).

All things work together for good

Now, when trouble threatens, or actually arrives, when disaster strikes the Christian, it is from this strong foundation that Paul argues: 'If God has freely loved me so much that he gave his only Son to die for me, then I can and will trust him in every circumstance." With John Newton he sings,

His love in time past
   Forbids me to think
He'll leave me at last
   In trouble to sink.[14]

Indeed, Paul goes further. Knowing that God loves him with an everlasting love, he interprets the troubles accordingly, believing that they will contribute to his final salvation. These are not random or accidental disasters, but God's method of preparing him for glory in heaven. *'And we know that in all things God works for the good of those who love him, who have been called according to his purpose'* (Romans 8:28). William Cowper[15], who had many deep troubles, advises the Christian:

Judge not the Lord by feeble sense,
   But trust him for his grace;
Behind a frowning providence
   He hides a smiling face.

---

14   *Begone unbelief*, hymn by John Newton (1725-1807).
15   Poet and friend of John Newton. Cowper suffered from severe mental illness.

Or again, in a less well-known hymn,

Trials must and will befall;
    But with humble faith to see
Love inscribed upon them all,
    This is happiness to me.[16]

Where the non-Christian treats sorrows as a reason for denying God's love, the Christian, who is absolutely convinced of God's love, sees them in a different light. His position is not changed by the troubles. To quote John Newton again,

Why should I complain
    Of want or distress,
Temptation or pain?
    He told me no less.[14]

He is-not immune to the pain or suffering; they hurt just as much as those of the non-Christian. However, he understands that sin has brought sorrow and suffering into the world, that it affects the whole of life and that Christians are not exempt from the common lot (1 Corinthians 10:13). So his faith in the love of God is not shaken, at least not if he has been taught properly beforehand. His idea of God's love did not involve the promise of a trouble-free life, so the arrival of trouble does not contradict his faith.

On the contrary, there is a benefit. Where the non-Christian feels, and indeed is, increasingly alone in his time of trouble, the Christian knows that the Lord is with him to comfort with his love and strengthen by his grace. Far from making him despair, the trouble draws him closer to his Lord. He argues in the opposite direction, not that a God of love could not allow this to happen, but that if he did not believe God was in it all, then he would despair. Now he 'sees love inscribed upon it all'. He may not know why, but he knows his God, the God of everlasting love.

This argument only applies to those who are believers, who have come to put their trust in the Lord. It is foolish to expect those who do not know and trust Christ to argue like this; indeed, it is

16   *Tis my happiness below*, hymn by William Cowper (1731-1800)

not true for them that *'all things work together for good'* (Romans 8:28). So I cannot hope to persuade you in a vacuum. However, there is surely enough here to demonstrate that if the gospel is true, then there is literally nothing that can happen to the Christian that is just cause to doubt God. Everything has been allowed for in the Bible's message, as Newton said.

The love of God which the Bible teaches is a love that embraces all the objections. It is only the pale imitations that people have invented that are contradicted by worldly events, which proves that they are counterfeit. The genuine article passes every test. This is why we had to begin by asking what God's love really is. The only solution for you, then, is to repent and believe the gospel. Then this knowledge and comfort of God's love can be yours.

7.
'I'm not that bad.'

When I was a student, a team from my college visited the local old people's home regularly and spoke to the old folk about the gospel of salvation. I was particularly taken with one elderly lady, who appeared genuinely interested in what we had to say. One day I thought we had made a real breakthrough. In conversation she made the admission:

'I know I'm not perfect.'

So I followed this up to make sure she realised what she was saying:

'So you admit that you're a sinner?' I said.

'Oh no!', she replied in a shocked voice, 'I'm not a sinner.'

This is not as illogical, or uncommon, as it might appear. Almost everybody would admit to not being perfect; that requires no humbling or abasement. They are just accepting that they are human like everybody else. But to say one is 'a sinner' implies to most people that one is inferior, not respectable, worthy of rejection by all 'decent' society. This she was not prepared to accept or admit. Nor are most people today.

Often, there is a sort of awareness of God's judgement and the need for salvation, but this only applies to other people—the dregs of society. It is all right to speak of drunks and addicts needing to be saved or converted or redeemed, but not 'decent people like us'!

'I'm not perfect, I agree, but I'm not that bad,'

i.e., so bad as to need saving. So the gospel of grace and salvation is not so much denied as dismissed as unnecessary; the good news is irrelevant.

'Please don't waste time on me; go and talk to the people who need your message, not us decent folk.'

This perception of ourselves as the 'decent folk', unlike the vandals, thugs and child-abusers, is the most effective obstacle to the gospel in the modern world—the most devastating hindrance to people's enjoyment of the blessing of God there is.

While it is commonplace to accuse churchgoers of being hypocrites and Pharisees, the fact is that today most of the Pharisees are outside the church. The people whom Jesus opposed—and who opposed Jesus—were those who denied that they needed a saviour.

'Go and talk to the tax collectors and sinners,' they would have said.

'There are plenty of people who need your message; go and convert them. Don't waste your time with us.'

They regarded themselves as the spiritually healthy ones who had no need of a doctor. In fact, they tried to have things both ways, for when Jesus did bother with the outcasts they condemned this as unsuitable behaviour for a religious teacher! See Luke 5:30-32.

So for an answer to this objection or dismissal we can turn to a parable that Jesus told about a Pharisee and a tax collector, regarded in those days as very much an outcast of society, a 'real sinner'.

To some who were confident of their own righteousness and looked down on everyone else, Jesus told this parable:

[10] *'Two men went up to the temple to pray, one a Pharisee and the other a tax collector.* [11] *The Pharisee stood by himself and prayed: "God, I thank you that I am not like other people –*

robbers, evildoers, adulterers – or even like this tax collector. [12] I fast twice a week and give a tenth of all I get."*

[13] *'But the tax collector stood at a distance. He would not even look up to heaven, but beat his breast and said, "God, have mercy on me, a sinner."*

[14] *'I tell you that this man, rather than the other, went home justified before God. For all those who exalt themselves will be humbled, and those who humble themselves will be exalted.'* (Luke 18:9-14)

This parable illustrates the basic mistakes that people make about themselves and their need.

Using a false standard

We are told, in matters of health and wealth, not to complain, because we can always find someone worse off than ourselves. It is equally, but less helpfully, true that in terms of goodness we can always find someone worse than ourselves. The Pharisee in the parable bolstered up his conviction of his own righteousness by comparing himself with the dregs of society, those known generally as 'sinners', i.e., outcasts and rejects like the swindling, Rome-loving, tax collectors, like the obvious criminals and those who made the headlines of the Sabbath newspapers.

So today people make the same error. We can all find people to look down on and regard as being really 'wicked'. Even those in prison take it upon themselves to 'punish' those who are guilty of crimes against children, even to murder them, as those who are beyond the pale, not respectable car thieves like themselves.

It is true that, from the merely human aspect, there is a difference between sinners. Not everyone is an Idi Amin or a Robert Maxwell, a serial killer or a child murderer. It is true, moreover, that Jesus himself distinguishes some parts of the law as being more important than others:

'Woe to you, teachers of the law and Pharisees, you hypocrites! You give a tenth of your spices – mint, dill and cumin. But you have neglected the more important matters of the law – justice, mercy and faithfulness. You should have practised the latter, without neglecting the former.' (Matthew 23:23).

There will also be degrees of punishment in hell, although it is clear that God's assessment of seriousness is often very different from ours. Nevertheless, when we think about our standing before God, none of these distinctions is relevant. According to the apostle Paul, quoting the Old Testament, *'There is no one righteous, not even one.'* (Romans 3:10) And, if you are unrighteous, you are under God's condemnation as a sinner. It makes no difference from this angle whether you are the worst or the least; a sinner is unrighteous and therefore condemned.

The standard is not other people, but God's law. According to the law of the land, a motorist whose blood has an alcohol content above the legal limit is guilty of an offence. It makes no difference that the next motorist is more drunk; both are guilty according to an absolute standard. In the same way everyone is guilty before God. *'Now we know that whatever the law says, it says to those who are under the law, so that every mouth may be silenced and the whole world held accountable to God. [20] Therefore no one will be declared righteous in God's sight by the works of the law; rather, through the law we become conscious of our sin'* (Romans 3:19-20).

It is often said that even if we obey 99% of the law and only fail on 1%, then we are guilty before God (Cf. James 2:10). This is certainly true, for the law is a unit, like a chain. There are no percentages; God's requirement is perfection. As we have seen already, if you break one link of a chain then the chain is broken and useless. However, this is really irrelevant as far as the non-Christian is concerned. No one gets anywhere near 99%. We do not have to search our record to find a sin here and a sin there. The Bible teaches that everything we do is sinful! (Isaiah 64:6)

We are basically rebels, outside God's kingdom and opposed to it in our hearts.

As rebels, all that we do is unacceptable to God. An enemy soldier may be a good husband, a good father and a respected citizen, but he is still an enemy. The fact that he is better than a criminal of that country is neither here nor there. We are unacceptable, not just this or that deed of ours.

In addition it is not just the obvious sins like theft or murder that count. First, we must reckon with sins against God. Even if it were true—and it never is—that 'I've never done anybody any harm', all have sinned directly against God:

'Love the Lord your God with all your heart and with all your soul and with all your mind and with all your strength.' (Mark 12:30)

He has a right to total obedience, wholehearted worship, a life lived entirely for his glory, love with all our heart and soul and mind and strength, and nobody at all ever keeps to this. Pharisees and tax collectors alike live for themselves.

Again, even in human terms of sin against our neighbour (Mark 12:31), there are sins of the heart and mind, like envy and hatred, that rank with the worst that men may do. Some people start from a far worse position, with great disadvantages of upbringing and background. Comparisons become quite irrelevant when all this is realised. I am not arguing that the blatant sinner is 'not so bad really', just a lovable rogue! The tax collector in the parable was undoubtedly a wicked man; he had it right:

'God, have mercy on me, a sinner.' (Luke 18:13)

The Pharisees were highly respected citizens; they were in many ways not as bad as the tax collectors, but they too were sinners in need of salvation. We are all 'that bad'.

Making a wrong assumption

After comparing himself with the tax collector and his ilk—very much to the latter's disadvantage—the Pharisee turns to his own positive merit. He lists his religious duties. He mentions his twice-weekly fasts, which went beyond anything the law of Moses required, and his giving away of a tenth of all he had, again more than the law demanded. In the same way many today not only regard themselves as being in a different category from 'sinners', but can also point to their good works of various kinds. For some it is religious activities like the Pharisee's: churchgoing, praying, giving to the poor; for others it is charitable deeds, being a good neighbour and so on.

Now let us be clear that the Pharisee actually did these things, just as his modern equivalent may do. Pharisees had a reputation with the common people for being really holy, rather like people today often admire monks and nuns. However, the New Testament makes it abundantly clear that we cannot earn God's approval by our good deeds of various kinds, whatever others may think. Apparently, the Pharisees, for all their emphasis on tithing (giving a tenth of their income), were very fond of money and, when Jesus told them they could not serve both God and Money (the god, 'Mammon'), they sneered at him. In reply he said, *'You are the ones who justify yourselves in the eyes of others, but God knows your hearts. What people value highly is detestable in God's sight.'* (Luke 16:15). God sees our hearts and understands our motives better than we do ourselves, never mind other people.

If we do 'good' things merely to impress our neighbours, or even to earn merit and salvation, then they are no longer good. Even if we are not insincere or merely showing off to gain the applause of others, the very idea of earning acceptance with God shows pride and self-righteousness, which are condemned in God's eyes.

Saul of Tarsus, later the apostle Paul, asserts that he lived according to his conscience, trying to gain a righteousness that would satisfy God. In fact, he thought he had done it! In his letter to the Philippians, chapter 3, he lists his assets: his birth, upbringing, education, theological qualifications and law-keeping, concluding that he was *'faultless'*. But he came to see that this was no use; he saw eventually that his covetousness disqualified him—and then realised that there was much more sin as well. In the end, he tells us, he counted all these supposed assets as rubbish, loss—a hindrance rather than a help when it came to acceptance with God, for they kept him from trusting in the perfect righteousness provided by God through Christ.

The proper time and place for good deeds of any kind is after we have believed and been forgiven and accepted by God's grace. We work, not 'for salvation' but, 'from salvation'. We love, worship, serve and glorify God because he loved us first (1 John 4:19). We do it from a grateful heart for what he has given us in Christ, not as a vain attempt to win his approval.

So, the right attitude before God is not the arrogant self-confidence of the Pharisee, but the humble shame of the tax collector. He does not merely acknowledge the truth of Romans 3:10—*'There is no one righteous'*—he feels it. He will not lift up his eyes to the throne of God; he beats his breast, not in a formal or outward show, but expressing the sorrow of his heart. He has been convicted of his sin.

Missing God's remedy

The result of judging by human standards and relying on one's own good deeds is not only failure; it is disaster. For those who take this position miss out on God's gracious remedy. The apostle Paul counted his supposed assets as 'loss', not just failure, because they prevented him from accepting Christ's righteousness:

– *⁴ though I myself have reasons for such confidence. If someone else thinks they have reasons to put confidence in the flesh, I have more: ⁵ circumcised on the eighth day, of the people of Israel, of the tribe of Benjamin, a Hebrew of Hebrews; in regard to the law, a Pharisee; ⁶ as for zeal, persecuting the church; as for righteousness based on the law, faultless.*

[7] But whatever were gains to me I now consider loss for the sake of Christ. (Philippians 3:4-7)

If we think we can save ourselves, even if we only mean making a contribution or trying our best with God's help, then we do not, and will not, ask God for his gracious free gift.

The Pharisee in the parable is a suitable example again: He asked for nothing. He simply told God what he did. He may even, as a Bible-teacher, like Nicodemus (John 3), have taught about the grace, mercy and love of God, but he did not need it himself, so he thought. Here we have come full circle. The counterpart of thinking yourself better than others is that you accept their need of grace, but deny it to yourself. The Pharisee, as long as he thought highly of himself, refused the gift from God.

In ordinary life there is a proud independence which is perhaps to be admired. Old people may resist offers to do things for them— kindly meant, but robbing them of their dignity. Sadly, however, this can go too far and they end up suffering unnecessarily. Spiritually there is no place for this at all. We have to admit that we are just as sinful and needy as the next man. We need to be saved just as much as the murderer, the adulterer, the thief. We are just as hopeless and helpless as addicts, indeed, often more hopeless, because they at least know they need help.

It is for this reason that the common people, the tax collectors and sinners listened to Jesus gladly. They knew they were sinners; they had no illusions about themselves. To them, he spoke of grace and mercy, of living water (John 4:11), of the bread of life (John 6:35). He offered forgiveness and renewal. Their only problem was whether it was too good to be true. Thus the tax collector in the parable simply pleads for mercy. The word he used means the removal of God's wrath and anger—the old word 'be propitiated'. He does not ask for help to be better, to improve his life. He does not even promise better for the future, although he would know that this must be so. He does not offer to make amends, although he knows that repentance is necessary. Nothing can contribute to his acceptance except God's mercy.

Is there, then, mercy and forgiveness apart from in the death of Christ? Some try to assert this, using—or rather misusing—this parable (Luke 18:9-14)) and that of the prodigal son (Luke 15). No parable gives the whole picture and we must remember that Christ was speaking before the crucifixion, to which he only referred at this time in a somewhat veiled way. Nevertheless it is probably significant that Jesus set his parable in the temple, the place of sacrifice. All the Jews knew that the way of receiving propitiation, the word the tax collector used, was by sacrifice. The Old Testament sacrifices pointed to the coming and dying of the Lord Jesus Christ. It is only through Christ, *'and him crucified'* (1 Corinthians 2:2), that there is forgiveness and mercy.

The parable concludes with the tax collector going home *'justified'*—accepted as righteous in God's eyes. What an amazing conclusion! Christ's hearers must have been astounded, just as the disciples were when he said how hard it was for a rich man to enter the kingdom of heaven (Matthew 19:23).

A tax collector justified, rather than a Pharisee! How can this be? The answer is simply that those who think they are 'not that bad' never see their need and never accept God's righteousness. Those who know there is nothing too bad to be said about them go to God and plead with him for mercy, for grace. They know they deserve nothing but God's punishment; they know they can earn nothing. But, accepting God's verdict on them, they also accept his remedy. The pride that tells us that we are 'not that bad' is the pride that insists on self-reliance and self-help, and which ends in self-destruction.

8.
'What about people who lived before Christ?'

This objection, of course, only arises in a certain context—that of the exclusiveness of Christianity. One of the favourite texts of Christian gospel-preachers and witnesses is John 14:6: *'Jesus answered, "I am the way and the truth and the life. No one comes to the Father except through me."'* The same assertion is made by the apostle Peter: *'Salvation is found in no one else, for there is no other name under heaven given to mankind by which we must be saved'* (Acts 4:12). It is this teaching that frequently produces the objection: 'What about those who lived before Christ, or', which amounts to the same thing in principle, 'those who have never heard of Christ, who were brought up in another religion, or even in none?'

The objection is really an accusation that God is unjust and unfair in condemning to hell those who have had no opportunity to believe the gospel. Such a God, it is alleged, is not worthy of worship, so they will not believe in him. Looked at another way, it is an assertion that since God is in fact just and fair, the gospel message is wrong; God does not condemn such people. Therefore, again, they will not believe the message. Sometimes the charge is joined to an assertion that God will not condemn and punish anybody at all, but this is to deny that God is just and is simply a denial of the Bible's teaching. For this chapter we will consider only the issue of the salvation of certain exceptional categories such as I have mentioned. In these instances there may appear to be a problem.

A false compromise

First, however, I must deal with an increasingly common approach to the subject by some Christians. They believe that the objection is valid to some extent and adjust the message accordingly. Some refer to so-called 'anonymous Christians', who, it is claimed, being sincere followers of another religion, are saved by Christ without actually trusting him. God, they say, accepts the sincerity of these people and applies his salvation to them just the same.[17] The Bible, however, speaks very definitely of being saved 'through faith'.

Others seize on certain biblical cases, like David and others in the Old Testament, i.e. before Christ, or Cornelius the Roman Centurion in Acts 10-11, to assert that there are some who are much more than sincere Muslims or good pagans. These people, it is maintained, come to an end of themselves and cry for mercy to God, without actually knowing about God's way of salvation through Christ crucified. So Cornelius is said to be a proof that God '*accepts men from every nation who fear him and do what is right*' (Acts 10:35). 'Surely', it is argued, 'God would not reject someone who pleads for mercy, simply because he has never heard of Christ?'

This is really a misunderstanding of the position both of Old Testament believers and of Cornelius. Faithful Jews before Christ did in fact believe in the promised Messiah/Christ[18]. They believed God's covenant promise of a Saviour and thus trusted the promised Christ for their salvation. Abraham is said to have believed and welcomed the promise *'from a distance'* (Hebrews 11:13). Moses' sacrifice of his position at the Egyptian court is described as accepting *'disgrace for the sake of Christ'* (Hebrews 11:26). God, who knew what was to happen, forgave them on the basis of the future sacrifice of Christ in whom they had believed. Cornelius was probably in this category, although he had not actually become a Jewish proselyte. Like Mary, Joseph, Simeon

---

17   Such as C.S. Lewis in *The Last Battle* (1956), where the fictional Emeth, the Calormene, describes his encounter with Aslan the lion.
18   Christ (Χριστος) being simply the Greek version of the Hebrew/Aramaic title 'Messiah'.

and Anna (Luke 1-2), he was waiting for the redemption of Israel by the Messiah, in whom he had put his faith, of which his 'fear' (Acts 10:2) was the evidence. On the other hand, it may be that he was not actually saved until Peter's visit, in which case we must notice that God made sure that he did, in fact, hear the gospel.

It has to be said that this theory begins from an entirely wrong premiss. Men are represented as seeking God, apparently of their own accord, on their own initiative, and putting God in a dilemma! Here are these people who have bypassed the proper channels and come seeking mercy. What is he to do? He is, so it seems, in something of a quandary! Now this misrepresents the whole situation. No one can come to the place of repentance apart from God; no one can humble himself for his sin in this way, as the theory requires, unless God enables him to do so. Now, if God has done this, will he not make sure that such a person also hears the gospel?

The biblical pattern is quite different. God has taken the initiative. He has chosen a people, whom Christ has redeemed and whom the Holy Spirit will bring to repentance and faith. In pursuance of this, God so orders all the circumstances that they do hear the gospel and believe. The scenario imagined by those who put the problematic idea forward will never happen. God has been known to bring men from a distant land to hear the message (Acts 8:27); he has sent missionaries or individual Christians to another land for just one convert.

The story of the Murut[19] tribe in Borneo illustrates the point. This tribe had become so degenerate before the Second World War that the Australian government decreed that they should be isolated and left to die out without corrupting others. No missionaries were allowed to go to them. However, some of these tribesmen went in the opposite direction, to the Indonesian part of the island, where they met with some Christians and brought back the gospel to their tribe. After the war it was

---

19   See https://en.wikipedia.org/wiki/Murut_people

discovered that many had been converted and the tribe transformed. God had his people among them and ensured that they heard the gospel. He predestines those whom he has chosen to be saved; that is to say, he ordains all the necessary means so that they will hear and, by his grace, believe and be saved.

Understanding the gospel

Instead of changing the message we should try to understand exactly what the gospel is saying. What do the texts I have quoted (John 14:6 and Acts 4:12) really mean? What does Christina Rossetti's hymn mean?

None other Lamb, none other name,
None other hope in heaven or earth or sea,
None other hiding-place from guilt and shame,
None beside thee.[20]

We can only be saved through Christ; there is no other way of access to God, no other way to heaven. Why?

This is not an arbitrary matter, as if God could accept us on some other basis but chooses not to, just to be awkward. The fact is that salvation is impossible by any other route. It is not that there are many bridges over the chasm, but God says only one is acceptable. Rather, there is only one bridge that actually reaches the other side. Many people try many others but are let down disastrously.

It is a question of sin and justice. Man's sin is such that a just and holy God cannot—I write with all reverence—cannot simply forgive. Many think of God as a kind of heavenly Father Christmas, who just lets people off the punishment because he feels generous, or, as someone like themselves, has to let people off because he is no better than they are. They overlook the fact that God is the Judge of the whole earth, the Ruler of the universe. In terms of human illustrations, we are not dealing with a father who remembers his own youthful misdeeds and is lenient accordingly, but a judge who represents the law of the land and is bound to administer it fairly and consistently. Many of the people who want God simply to ignore sin get very upset if earthly magistrates do just that, especially if their own property is involved.

So the position of the Bible is that salvation is by faith alone, because it is through Christ crucified alone, and faith is the only way to make that Saviour and his salvation mine. The exclusive character of the gospel is not arbitrary but just, not unkind but fair. In any case, who needs more than one way of salvation, so long as it works? It is not really the exclusiveness that offends, but the nature of that one way. People do not want this way; it offends their pride and upsets their way of life.

There is a way for man to rise
To that sublime abode,
An offering and a sacrifice,
A Holy Spirit's energies,
An Advocate with God.[21]

Judgement and knowledge

The next step in the objection argues that it is unfair to condemn people who have never heard the gospel, to blame them for not crossing a bridge that they have never seen or heard of. This seems a very fair complaint, except, of course, that in some cases they could know about the gospel if they took the trouble to find out, especially in this country. Ignorance of the law is no excuse, we are told; it is our responsibility to find out.

However, if we think of those who have been born in a time or place where they could not find out or hear the gospel, then we have to accept this objection in principle. Indeed, the Bible itself asserts the principle of relative responsibility. *'From everyone who has been given much, much will be demanded; and from the*

---

21   Thomas Binney (1798–1874), an English Congregationalist divine

one who has been entrusted with much, much more will be asked' (Luke 12:48).

No one will be condemned for not believing what he has not heard. No one will go to hell merely because he has not believed the gospel he never heard. Some evangelists unwittingly lead people astray by asserting that the only thing that really matters is our response to Jesus Christ in the gospel, that such unbelief is the only sin that condemns. This is not so. Although people may not know the gospel, and therefore not be responsible to obey it, they do know other things and are responsible to believe and obey those. If they fail here they are condemned as guilty sinners. The previous verses in Luke 12 gives some understanding of this: *'The servant who knows the master's will and does not get ready* [i.e., for his master's return] *or does not do what the master wants will be beaten with many blows. ⁴⁸ But the one who does not know and does things deserving punishment will be beaten with few blows.'* (Luke 12:47-48) Thus the Bible itself teaches the principle of proportionate responsibility, but it does not let people off the hook altogether.

Everyone knows something about God and his will—enough to know they must worship and obey him. The apostle Paul spends some time in his letter to the Romans explaining this, before he comes to the gospel: *'The wrath of God is being revealed from heaven against all the godlessness and wickedness of people, who suppress the truth by their wickedness, ¹⁹ since what may be known about God is plain to them, because God has made it plain to them. ²⁰ For since the creation of the world God's invisible qualities – his eternal power and divine nature – have been clearly seen, being understood from what has been made, so that people are without excuse.'* (Romans 1:18-20).

He goes on to explain that men *'did not think it worthwhile to retain the knowledge of God'* (v.28). He adds, in verse 32, that *'Although they know God's righteous decree that those who do such things deserve death, they not only continue to do these very things but also approve of those who practise them.'* He argues too, from the workings of conscience, that even non-Jews have *'the requirements of the law ... written on their hearts'* (Romans 2:15).

They all, therefore, know enough to be condemned, to be without excuse, although they do not know enough to be saved. That requires a knowledge of the gospel, so the Christian preacher or witness seeks to build on this basic knowledge. He does not need to 'prove' the existence of God by intellectual and logical argument. Indeed, the so-called traditional 'proofs' do not achieve very much; at best they can only show that the existence of some supreme being is possible or, perhaps, probable. The Bible, however, tells us that, because he is made in the image of God, any human really knows that God, the true God, exists. He may suppress this (Romans 1:18), but he knows it in his heart and we can work on this assumption.

This does not mean that atheists and agnostics are liars or are merely pretending. They have been so blinded by sin and conditioned by their upbringing and environment that they think they are being honest and scientific. The Bible, however, is quite clear, and the evidence of 'primitive' tribes and people's reaction under stress—how many pray to the God in whom they do not believe! —as well as their sense of right and wrong, and their acceptance of some absolutes when they themselves are the victims of crime, no matter what they profess in theory, all tend to confirm that they know there is a God.

It is for their refusal to believe and obey what they know of God's will that people will be condemned. Rejecting the gospel, if they hear it, only adds to their guilt. The fundamental sin for which they are judged is disobedience and rebellion against the God they do know in this sense discussed. It is like someone who dies from a disease for which there is a cure, but one which is not available in that country. In a sense he dies because he does not have the remedy, but it is still the disease that kills him. So it is with the heathen who has never heard the gospel. In a sense he dies because he does not have the gospel, but in fact it is his sin which brings condemnation. And this is just.

Once we assert that God is just, we come up against more objections, all based on what people think God ought to do. He ought to forgive everybody; he ought to save everybody; he ought to cause the gospel to be made known everywhere, etc. However, we cannot lay down what the Creator of the world ought to do. He says what ought to be and what he does is inherently just. He is holy and pure, and whatever he decides will be just and right. Paul asserts, in the same context as the verses I have just been quoting, that *'God's judgement against those who do such things is based on truth'* (Romans 2:2). Centuries before, Abraham could plead with confidence before God, *'Will not the Judge of all the earth do right?'* (Genesis 18:25).

This is not secret or arbitrary. On the Day of Judgement what God has done will be seen to be just. His judgement of people will be *'according to what they* [have] *done'* (Revelation 20:12,13; 22:12), in other words, based on the evidence, so that justice will be seen to be done. Even those who are saved by grace through faith will be seen to be holy and righteous, worthy, because God has made them worthy, to enter heaven. The deeds which could never save them will provide ample evidence of the reality of their faith, and God will finally make them fit for his presence. Conversely, the deeds of unbelievers will show conclusively that they have not lived up to the light that they had. For Christians this is a great source of comfort. There are many situations that we do not understand, many people whose apparent fate seems dubious or even unfair to us, but we can be sure, in fact, that everything is just and that the Last Day will show this clearly.

More immediately relevant, is the question of what we do here and now. For the Christian, all this makes clear and urgent his responsibility to make the gospel known everywhere to as many as possible. This is their only hope. I am not allowed to use the Bible's teaching about the sovereignty of God as an excuse for laxity and laziness. God has ordained that people be saved by the appropriate means. I must make the gospel freely available to all.

More relevant in the context of this book is the responsibility of everyone to respond to the message they have heard. It will be no defence on the Day of Judgement to say, 'What about those who never heard?' Your own responsibility is to obey what you have heard—the gospel of Jesus Christ. What are you going to do about it?

When some of his hearers asked Jesus how many would be saved, he did not give a direct answer. Instead he exhorted them, *'Make every effort to enter through the narrow door, because many, I tell you, will try to enter* [when it is too late] *and will not be able'* (Luke 13:24).

It may seem that to argue in this way is hard and unfeeling. If we Christians do give that impression then we must ask pardon, for our God does not intend it in that way. To put the blame for their own fate on those who have not heard, because of their sin, is merely to treat them as responsible human beings, not as robots or pawns. Nor should we be callous and uncaring; our Lord is neither of these things. Jesus himself grieved over Jerusalem: *'How often I have longed to gather your children together, as a hen gathers her chicks under her wings, and you were not willing.'* (Luke 13:34). He even wept over the doomed city as he went there to be crucified (Luke 19:41).

The mark of the real Christian is that instead of debating and doubting the wisdom and justice of God, he gets on with making the gospel known. The mark of the sincere seeker is that he trusts God and makes sure of his salvation by repenting of his sin. *'He who has ears, let him hear'* (Matthew 13:9).

9.
'But I don't want to change my lifestyle.'

When all is said and done, there remain the people who simply do not want to pay the price of becoming a Christian. This may seem strange in a day when preachers in general do not stress this aspect of the gospel message. Indeed, the more usual mistake is not to count the cost at all.

Failure to count the cost

In this case people leap without looking, start to build without thinking about what it will cost, as Jesus described in Luke 14:28-30: *'Suppose one of you wants to build a tower. Won't you first sit down and estimate the cost to see if you have enough money to complete it? [29] For if you lay the foundation and are not able to finish it, everyone who sees it will ridicule you, [30] saying, "This person began to build and wasn't able to finish."'*

The countryside is littered with 'follies', buildings so called be-cause they are monuments to the folly of the builder, who either built something pointless, or had to leave his work incomplete because he ran out of money. The church landscape, also, is full of such tragic remains—people who claimed that they had become Christians, but had not counted the cost and came to grief when persecution arose or the way became hard for some other reason, when the price became too high.

Jesus' parable of the sower (Matthew 13:3-9,18-23) describes such cases. Using the picture of the seed, representing the '*word*' of the gospel, he describes how some seeds spring up very quickly, but when the sun rises they shrivel up, because they do not have deep roots. Such is the case of those who rush into a profession of faith without pausing to think and count. Others are represented by seed sown among thorns. Again disaster follows when the thorns grow and choke the seedlings. These are people who have not realised that Christ's way demands a new life and the pull of riches or the drag of this world's cares soon stifles them.

True, such people were not really Christians in the first place, but they thought they were, and often become very embittered, saying, 'I tried it and it didn't work.' They may, in fact, have good cause for complaint, not against God, but against the evangelist who, in his eagerness to gain converts, did not make clear the cost that is involved in becoming a Christian. It may be, of course, that they simply did not listen, as the parable implies. This is why it is so important for Christians to make clear to enquirers and interested thinkers that there is a price to pay.

The necessity of counting the cost

In fact, many people can put two and two together. They see how Christians live and realise that their lifestyle is very different from that of the rest of the world. So they count the cost and come to the wrong conclusion, like the student mentioned earlier, whose only fear was that the gospel might prove to be true and thus require a change in his lifestyle which he was unwilling to make. He had grasped the fact that you cannot become a Christian and live in the same way as before. The trouble is that he, like many others who have done their sums, had got the answer wrong. The Bible's teaching, especially that of the Lord Jesus Christ, points in the opposite direction.

In the same chapter which contains the parable of the sower, we find two more parables, which are relevant to our subject:

The kingdom of heaven is like treasure hidden in a field. When a man found it, he hid it again, and then in his joy went and sold all he had and bought that field.

Again, the kingdom of heaven is like a merchant looking for fine pearls. When he found one of great value, he went away and sold everything he had and bought it. (Matthew 13:44-46)

The first parable is about someone who comes upon the good news unawares and, like C. S. Lewis, is 'surprised by joy'; the other is about a man who is actually looking for it, perhaps someone with a religious upbringing. But the point is the same: the kingdom of God is worth any sacrifice to get hold of it. The kingdom of heaven is extremely costly, but it is infinitely valuable —and the contrast in these two adverbs (extremely and infinitely) is both deliberate and significant. In each case the man had to sell all that he had, but in each case also he gained something beyond price.

Infinitely valuable

Oscar Wilde defined a cynic as someone who knows the price of everything and the value of nothing[22]. When we do our kingdom sums, we must look first and carefully at the value of Christ's kingdom. What he is referring to is the whole of what is offered in the good news of the gospel. Jesus uses the pictures of treasure and pearls here; elsewhere the Bible speaks of riches and feasts. The proper response to the gospel message is joy, not the superficial glee of the parable of the sower, but the deep, thoughtful and lasting joy of the parable of the treasure. We shall have to consider in due course that the Christian way is narrow, but from the present perspective the stress is on the wonder and glory of the salvation that Christ gives.

It is quite wrong to give the impression, as some gloomy Christians do, that the gospel is bad news rather than the good news that the word[23] means! We are gravely at fault if we are miserable all the time and imply that nothing else is to be expected. Please do not be put off. The New Testament is full of references to joy and rejoicing, even in the midst of trials and

22   *Lady Windemere's Fan*, a play by Oscal Wilde, first performed 1892.
23   'Gospel' is Old English for good news.

suffering. Do you remember the Thessalonians in chapter 4? (1 Thessalonians 1:6) This can only be because of something beyond the trial and suffering that more than compensates—that is, 'the boundless riches of Christ' (Ephesians 3:8).

It is hard, indeed impossible, to give an adequate description of the blessings that we Christians have through faith in Jesus Christ, although much of this must have become clear already in this book. In chapter 4 we looked at some of the characteristics of a religion that is worth having. Christianity is such a religion: it provides a purpose in life, a new power to live life and, especially, a clear conscience through the forgiveness of sins. The Christian enjoys the love of God and the peace and joy that flow from this. These riches may be summed up as all that belongs to salvation from sin: its guilt, its power and, ultimately, even its corruption.

As well as this central privilege of our relationship to God, there are all the benefits that the Christian receives in terms of satisfaction, peace of mind, hope and joy, and also from fellowship with God's people, and the loving help they give to their brothers and sisters in Christ. It is largely this that Jesus must have intended when he assured Peter that those who had given up anything for him—'houses or brothers or sisters ... fields'—would receive back 'a hundred times as much' (Matthew 19:29). Then he added that they would also 'inherit eternal life'. Essentially, Christians are to be envied because they have the promise of eternal life and the certainty that they have been saved from the wrath of God and, consequently, from hell. Whatever sceptics may say, and however much they may sneer about 'pie in the sky when you die', this is the great certainty that controls the Christian in his thinking about the 'down-side' of his faith.

We may divide the blessings into those we already have in our experience, like justification and adoption, and those which are yet to come, although they are already sure and certain because of God's promises. The apostle John puts the two side by side when he writes, 'See what great love the Father has lavished on *us, that we should be called children of God! And that is what we are! ...* [2] *Dear friends, now we are children of God, and what we will be has not yet been made known. But we know that when Christ appears, we shall be like him, for we shall see him as he is.'* (1 John 3:1-2).

At the end of another of Jesus' parables, he contrasts the fate of the unbeliever—*'the blazing furnace, where there will be weeping and gnashing of teeth'*—with the destiny of the Christian: *'Then the righteous will shine like the sun in the kingdom of their Father'* (Matthew 13:42-43). Surely this contrast enables us to value eternal life properly!

Extremely costly

However, this is not the whole picture. There is a price that has to be paid, and unless we are prepared for this it comes as a devastating and often fatal shock, which leads to a professing Christian giving up his 'faith'. The parables speak of 'selling' and 'buying' to convey this idea, but we must be quite clear what is not being said. The parables are talking about what we might call the mechanics of salvation, the psychology of conversion, not merit and deserts. They must not be interpreted, in defiance of the rest of the Bible, to mean that we earn our salvation. Salvation is a free gift; justification is through faith alone. However, the actual obtaining of this free gift demands an effort.

Thus Christ elsewhere warns enquirers that they must 'strive' or *'make every effort to enter through the narrow door'* (Luke 13:24). He encourages people to seek so that they may find. The picture is of a man offering free food to a starving multitude. It is a gift, but those at the back of the crowd must fight their way through to obtain their share. If they just sit and wait they will receive nothing. They do not earn it; they do not merit it, but without making the effort they will not get it.

Basically we may say that the blessings of the kingdom are for disciples. Believers are called to be disciples, not parasites, and this starts right from the beginning. The way into the kingdom is hard for sinful man; the door truly is small and the way is narrow (Matthew 7:14). This is why it is so necessary to count the cost first. The cost begins with the humbling that has to take place for a proud sinner to accept that his good deeds are of no value, and that he must receive salvation as a free gift or not at all. At the close of his parable about the Pharisee and the tax collector, Jesus added the warning: *'For all those who exalt themselves will be humbled, and those who humble themselves will be exalted.'* (Luke 18:14). Only those who adopt the low position of the supplicant, the beggar, can receive the gift. The gate is *'small'*.

Nevertheless, we must not ignore the rest of the verse. Those *'who humble themselves will be exalted'*; it will be infinitely worth their while. This is not to suggest that the humbling is a mere pretence to gain the exaltation, but the blessing does really follow. This is what I mean by doing the sums properly. We must always count both columns of the ledger; the credit column far outweighs the debit side. In the same way it is vital to remember that although the door is *'narrow'*, it leads to life, eternal life, whereas the broad road leads to destruction. No assessment of the situation is accurate unless it takes both sides into account (Matthew 7:13-14).

Self-denial

Self-denial begins with the humbling that I have already dealt with, but it also continues as an essential part of discipleship. Saying 'No' to ourselves and our desires is not some kind of masochism or enjoying suffering, but a deliberate subordination of our wishes to the will of God. No matter what it costs in 'giving up', the Christian has to obey God's command now that he is a disciple. This is expressed by the extreme words of Matthew 5:29-30: *'If your right eye causes you to sin, gouge it out and throw it away. It is better for you to lose one part of your body than for your whole body to be thrown into hell.'* Here, Jesus is not encouraging self-mutilation, but putting in striking form his demand for radical obedience, whatever it may cost. In this case it means restricting the use of our eyes and even missing out on some of the legitimate things that we might look at, so that we do not sin, but the principle extends more widely.

This self-denial extends even to the actual losing of life for the sake of Christ, by being faithful even to death in persecution. Matthew 16:24-26 describes this: *'Whoever wants to be my disciple must deny themselves and take up their cross and follow me.'* The cross for a believer is not just any kind of trouble, like an illness or a burdensome situation, but strictly accepting persecution which comes through being faithful to Christ. Notice the 'must': this is not optional; it is part of the price.

Then, however, Jesus adds the 'but', which makes it all worthwhile: *'For whoever wants to save their life[footnote 24] will lose it, but whoever loses their life for me will find it. [26] What good will it be for someone to gain the whole world, yet forfeit their life[footnote 24]? Or what can anyone give in exchange for their life[footnote 24]?'*

Consider eternity

The validity of this argument and motivation depends on the reality of the contrast between time and eternity. Loss in this world is more than compensated for by gain in the life to come. Why? Because the quality as well as the length of eternity—if this is the right way to think of it—is so much greater than anything in this world. This is the difference between 'extremely costly' and 'infinitely valuable'.

The apostle Paul argues in the same way in a couple of places. In Romans 8:18 he writes, *'I consider that our present sufferings are not worth comparing with the glory that will be revealed in us.'* This, of course, depends on the quality of the glory that he is referring to, so he goes on to describe the glorious liberty of the children of God, their life in a renewed universe with God. Even more striking are his words in 2 Corinthians 4:17: *'For our light*

---

24   Taking the NIV margin here. See p.105ff of *The Right End of the Stick*, also from *Covenant Books UK* for a discussion of how this kind of verse should be translated.

and momentary troubles are achieving for us an eternal glory that far outweighs them all.'

In later chapters he describes these *'light'* afflictions (2 Corinthians 4:17); they include *'troubles, hardships and distresses ... beatings, imprisonments and riots'* (2 Corinthians 6:4-5). He describes how, in contrast with certain impostors, he has *'worked much harder, been in prison more frequently, been flogged more severely, and been exposed to death again and again. [24] Five times I received from the Jews the forty lashes minus one. [25] Three times I was beaten with rods, once I was pelted with stones, three times I was shipwrecked,'* and so on (2 Corinthians 11:23-28).

How can he describe these afflictions as *'light'*? He compares them with the positive blessings of being with Christ for ever. In the same way he can describe his lifelong troubles as *'momentary'* (2 Corinthians 4:17) by comparing them with eternity: *'So we fix our eyes not on what is seen, but on what is not seen. For what is seen is temporary, but what is not seen is eternal'* (2 Corinthians 4:18).

We are often told that everything is relative. This is not true; there are many absolutes for the Christian. In this case, however, it is true. If we compare the cost of being a Christian with the cost of living a self-centred life, then the latter appears very expensive indeed. If we compare it with the price we would pay in eternity, then it seems very little.

Three quotations

1. Polycarp was a disciple of the apostle John, who after serving Christ for eighty-six years was condemned to die for his faith. When they threatened him with being burned to death, he replied, 'You threaten me with the fire that burns for an hour and in a little while is put out, for you do not know about the fire of the

judgement to come, and the eternal punishment reserved for the ungodly.' [25]

2. Jim Elliott was a missionary to the Auca Indians in Ecuador and was murdered by the men he had gone to help. Seven years earlier he had declared his faith: 'He is no fool who gives what he cannot keep, to gain what he cannot lose.'

Jim Elliot's personal journal
reproduced from Wikimedia Commons.

3. Dr Martyn Lloyd-Jones left a brilliant medical career early last century to become a preacher of the gospel in a poor part of South Wales. When asked about what he had sacrificed his answer was: 'I gave up nothing; I received everything.' [26] Here the same comparative principle applies. What he gave up was, in actual fact, very much. In the light of eternity it was nothing at all.

If after all this you still are unwilling to give up your old way of life, it can only be because you have not yet seen your sin and the judgement of God—that is, because you have not yet realised the cost of not becoming a Christian.

25   *The Martyrdom of Polycarp.* Translated by J.B. Lightfoot. 1990 Athena Data Products: http://www.earlychristianwritings.com/text/martyrdompolycarp-lightfoot.html, accessed 26/05/2022.

26   *The Life of D. Martyn Lloyd-Jones,* 1899-1981, by Iain Murray, Banner of Truth, 2013.

10.
'I don't know what to do.'

It is wrong to think that becoming a Christian is necessarily a complicated matter. It is only the differences between people's temperament and experience, combined with the need to correct some false ideas, that might make it a complicated business.

On the other hand, it is important not to reduce it, rather simplistically, to outward forms; one does not simply sign on the dotted line and pay the subscription, like joining a human club. Becoming a Christian is really what God does for us and to us. It is recorded in Acts 2:47 that *'The Lord added to their number daily those who were being saved.'* We must, therefore, distinguish between the simplicity of the way—faith—and the depth and complexity of the experience, which varies immensely from person to person. Many false conversions arise from ignoring these matters.

Preparing the ground

For instance, the question, "What must I do to be saved?' was put at various times either to Jesus himself or to the apostles (Acts 16:30). The answer that was given depended on the actual position of the enquirer and on what he really meant. Some were nearer to becoming Christians than others (Mark 12:34) and Jesus, especially, answered in the light of this, since he knew exactly 'where they were coming from', as modern parlance has it.

Some certainly thought that by doing something they could earn their way into the kingdom of God and were answered accordingly. Thus the ruler who asked Jesus, 'What must I do to inherit eternal life?' was directed to the Ten Commandments and then, specifically, to 'Sell everything you have and give to the poor,' not just because he could save himself by obeying, but because he needed to realise that he had far too superficial an idea of sin, especially his idolatrous worship of riches. In his case Jesus took him back a step so that he could see the gospel more clearly. It was at the end of this conversation (Luke 18:18-30) that Jesus told his disciples that even such a person could be saved, because, *'What is impossible with man is possible with God.'* (Luke 18:27) The ruler had to be changed before he could enter the kingdom.

Another 'expert in the law' (Luke 10:25), who asked what he must do to inherit eternal life, was also pointed to the commandments and then told the parable of the Good Samaritan. This has been misunderstood, as if it were saying that we can save ourselves by copying the Samaritan. The proper meaning is that the real evidence of being one of God's people is loving others like that. It is obvious that the questioner was assuming that all Jews, like the priest and the Levite in the parable, qualified automatically.

What must I do to be saved?

In all these cases, and others like them, there is implicit in the question the idea that we have to do something ourselves to be saved—in other words, to merit or earn salvation and eternal life. Nowhere is this taught in the Bible. Salvation is all by grace through faith; it is received as a free gift or not at all. If this is not understood, then we must take note of Jesus' procedure and go back a stage until we are sure that we are such helpless sinners that we cannot save ourselves, but can only be saved by God's grace through the cross of Christ.

Although there is no necessary preparatory step, which gives us the right to believe, it is a simple, practical fact that, unless we see our sin and need properly, and understand our helplessness to save ourselves, we shall not believe properly either. When we have come to this point, we can ask the question in the right way: 'How do I actually come into possession of this free gift? How can I know that I am one of those saved by the grace of God?'

Thus, when the jailer at Philippi asks the apostle Paul, "What must I do to be saved?' (Acts 16:30) and is clearly in earnest because he has been convicted of his grievous sin against God, he is given a simple gospel answer: *'Believe in the Lord Jesus, and you will be saved.'* (Acts 16:31) The preparatory work has been done, by God, and he is ready to receive the clear direction that he needs to become a Christian.

Before we look at this in more detail, we must repeat that it is wrong to lay down outward procedures and methods of 'making a decision'. These are not only unnecessary; they can be harmful by diverting attention from what really has to be done. Thus there is no set form of words which has to be followed; there is no action which has to be performed, such as going out to the front of a meeting; even baptism must not be confused with faith; there is no outward sign, like putting up a hand or signing a card, which can replace or represent faith.

And insofar as these things mean overcoming embarrassment and the fear of others, they can divert attention from the proper 'decision', which is to come to Christ, to a purely natural 'decision' to do this or that. Someone sitting in a meeting may be interested in becoming a Christian, but may have his mind turned to the issue of whether he dare go out to the front, and so the real, spiritual challenge disappears. Those who do actually respond by doing one of these things may regard themselves as converted, when in fact they have only done something on an earthly level and not before God at all. Do not be diverted into looking for something like that, or be content with doing it. That is the way of false conversion.

Faith

There is a danger of turning faith into a good deed or 'work', as if faith itself had some inherent power which causes us to be saved. In the Gospels we are given many illustrations of people coming to Christ to be healed. They are sometimes told, *'Your faith has healed you'* (e.g. Matthew 9:22). Clearly, what this means is that Jesus has healed them through their faith; their faith is the channel, through which Christ's power has come to them. We must not have faith in our faith. Faith is only the instrument by which we receive God's gift, the empty hand into which God places his salvation.

Equally, we must be clear that there is no such thing as faith on its own; it is always faith in something or someone. Too often today faith is taken to mean a kind of wishful thinking, a hoping for the best in difficult circumstances. 'Oh well,' says the troubled person, 'I suppose we must just have faith,' meaning that he or she must hold on desperately in the hope that all will turn out well in the end. In the Bible it is faith in the gospel, or faith in Christ, or God.

What, then, does it mean to believe in the Lord Jesus to be saved? There are three elements in faith (or believing—it is the same word in the original language): knowledge, assent and trust. All are necessary; it is fatal to omit one aspect, however sincere you may be. Definitions are often cold and not always easy to understand. We can, however, gain help from the many occasions in the Gospels when people come to Christ for healing of the body. In Christ's ministry this was a picture of the salvation of the soul and their faith is a picture of saving faith resulting in eternal life. We can see all three elements in the case of the two blind men whose sight Christ restored.

'As Jesus went on from there, two blind men followed him, calling out, 'Have mercy on us, Son of David!'

When he had gone indoors, the blind men came to him, and he asked them, 'Do you believe that I can do this?'

"Yes, Lord,' they replied.

Then he touched their eyes and said, 'According to your faith will it be done to you'; and their sight was restored.'
(Matthew 9:27-30)

1. Knowledge

Faith is often misunderstood as trying hard to believe something that is illogical or even untrue. The contrary is true in the Bible. Faith is believing what we have good authority for accepting as true. It is based on knowledge. For instance, in Romans 10:17, Paul writes that *'Faith comes from hearing the message, and the message is heard through the word about Christ.'* We do not believe anything we want to believe; we believe what we have heard in the gospel.

So, when people came to Jesus for healing, they knew about him, his claims, his power and his reputation. The blind men, who were told, *'According to your faith let it be done to you'* (Matthew 9:29), addressed him as *'Son of David'* (Matthew 9:27), i.e., the Messiah, the Saviour they were expecting to come. They would know that one of the signs of the Messiah was that he would give sight to the blind (Isaiah 35:5) and, probably, that he had done just that already. They called out, *'Have mercy on us!'* because they knew that God's blessings are not earned, but given in mercy and grace.

In the same way, there has to be knowledge of the gospel. Faith is not a vague feeling that perhaps God will be merciful; it is based on the knowledge of what God has said in the gospel message. It is based on what God has said about his Son, about the meaning of the cross, about the way of salvation through grace and mercy, not merit.

Included in this knowledge, of course, is awareness of our sin and need, just as the blind men realised their need of healing, having no doubts about their blindness. This is why Jesus had to deal severely with the men we considered earlier (see chapter 9 on counting the cost).

On the other hand, when people say, "I believe God will be merciful and forgive everybody," that is not faith; it is not based on the truth of the gospel; it is their own unjustified supposition or hope.

2. Assent

Next comes assent, or believing that the gospel is true. The two blind men were asked, *'Do you believe that I am able to do this?'* (Matthew 9:28) They replied that they did. In the previous chapter, a leper came to Jesus and showed this same kind of faith by saying, *'Lord, if you are willing, you can make me clean'* (Matthew 8:2). In the same way, the man or woman coming to Christ for salvation must be able to say that he or she believes that Jesus is the Son of God and that he can forgive sins (Matthew 9:6), and that he does show mercy to sinners. They must believe the gospel.

Some, of course, stop here and that is very dangerous. It is not enough just to accept 'the church's teaching' and think that you are safe. Assent is necessary but never sufficient. There are many examples in the New Testament of people who 'believed' in Jesus (e.g. Simon the Sorcerer in Acts 8:13ff), which meant that they accepted his claims to be the Messiah—what has been called 'historic faith'. These same people (Cf. Matthew 21:8-9, 27:20-26) are shown later calling for the death of Christ. They were clearly not genuinely converted. There are many who reject the ideas of the Jehovah's Witnesses, or are horrified that some bishops and others do not really believe in the resurrection or the virgin birth of Christ. At the same time they show no awareness of sin, no signs of grace in their lives, no holiness or devotion to Christ. They have just this historic faith and no more.

If this assent to the gospel is real, it will lead to something else— that is, trust. So, in Romans 10:9, after stating that *'If you confess with your mouth, "Jesus is Lord," and believe in your heart that God raised him from the dead, you will be saved,'* Paul goes on in verse 11 to quote, *'Anyone who believes in him will never be put to shame.'* If you really believe the gospel *'in your heart'*, not just with the intellect, but with a heartfelt conviction, including conviction of sin, then you will go on to personal trust in the Saviour.

3. Trust

There has to be a personal encounter with Christ. You can believe 'that Christ died for your sins', as some evangelists carelessly urge, and much else, and still be lost. That is not saving faith. No doubt, just as the demons believe that there is one God (James 2:19), so they will accept that Christ died for sinners. They do not, however, trust Christ for themselves.

What does it mean to trust Christ? Again definitions are not very helpful, but the Gospel record is. What we find there is men and women actually coming to Christ and asking for mercy, pleading for him to make them whole (i.e. to save them).

The two blind men pleaded, *'Have mercy on us.'* (Matthew 9:27) They persevered until Christ paid attention to them and granted them what they wanted and needed.

The ill woman, also in Matthew 9 (20-22), who believed that Christ could heal her, showed her faith by touching the edge of his cloak. This was not superstition, but an awareness that believing mechanically is no good; we must have personal dealings with the Saviour if we are to benefit from his grace and power.

The word for believing can in some settings mean to 'entrust'. Thus in John 2:23 we find people who *'believed in his name'*. This, it becomes clear, was only assent, historic faith, for we are immediately told that Jesus *'would not entrust himself to them'*. (John 2:24) The word translated 'entrust' is simply the word for 'believe' or 'trust'. The sinner who knows he is lost and condemned for his sin, but believes the message of the gospel, entrusts himself to Christ; he entrusts his soul and its salvation to the one who *'is able to save completely those who come to God through him'* (Hebrews 7:25). This entrusting is expressed in coming to Christ in person, like the ill people in the Gospels.

Christ is a risen, living Saviour, not a dead one. We can communicate with him when we speak to him. The prophet Hosea tells us how to come to him in prayer:

Take words with you
    and return to the Lord.
Say to him:
'Forgive us all our sins
    and receive us graciously.' (Hosea 14:2)

I am not advocating a set form of words, but Hosea does give us the right idea. If you have seen your sin and feel it keenly; if you are truly sorry and want to be forgiven and saved, you will not need words to be put into your mouth. It will be enough to be pointed in the right direction. You will not need someone to pray for you; you will want to go yourself to the one who can save you.

What about repentance?

Did not Peter tell the people who were convicted of their sin on the Day of Pentecost to 'repent'? Is this not necessary? In spite of some who seem to think that repenting is a 'work', we must assert that it certainly is necessary. Christ warned his hearers that unless they repented they would all perish (Luke 13:3,5). Paul told the Athenians that God now *'commands all people everywhere to repent'* (Acts 17:30).

Those who come to Christ come to him as Lord. They entrust themselves to him as Lord as well as Saviour. They can do nothing else, for he is both, indivisibly. We cannot have Christ as Saviour only. We have to believe in Jesus Christ as Lord, and that means repentance.

We have really dealt with this already (see chapter 2), but to summarise, repentance means a radical change of mind and heart and attitude, which leads to a transformed life. In the New Testament it is more or less equivalent to being converted or turning (or returning) to God. This is what I have just been describing. It is not just feeling sorry for your sins, although that is involved; many do that but soon lose their convictions. Repentance brings us back to God; it turns us round in our tracks. We admit we were wrong; we cease our rebellion and humble ourselves before the Saviour.

Repentance is the other side of the coin labelled 'faith'. If you believe the gospel, you have changed your mind about it—and about yourself, about God and about salvation.

If you trust the Saviour, then you have changed your attitude to your own works and goodness—your old, imagined ability to save yourself. If you entrust yourself to the Lord Jesus Christ, then you have stopped your rebellion and changed your allegiance by returning to the Lord.

This is not to minimise the importance of repentance in any way, but just as the Bible sometimes demands repentance and does not mention faith (Luke 24:47; Acts 2:38), so on other occasions it demands faith and does not mention repentance (Acts 16:31). This can only be because real faith includes repentance, and real repentance includes faith. You cannot have the one without the other.

Persevere

The two blind men have one last lesson for us. It seems that, at first, Jesus paid no attention to them, but they carried on following him and even went into the house to secure healing (Matthew 9:27-28). This fits with the exhortation that he himself gave in Luke 13:24. He was speaking to some people who were raising an objection, in the form of a question, about how many would be saved.

To such a theoretical question he gave no answer, but pointed out their danger and their responsibility for securing their own salvation: *'Make every effort to enter* [the kingdom] *through the narrow door, because many, I tell you, will try to enter and will not be able to.'* This inability to enter does not refer to God's unwillingness to allow them in, but, as the next verse makes clear, to those who leave it too late.

Meanwhile, the narrowness of the door tells us that there are difficulties and obstacles in the way that have to be overcome. This is not to earn the salvation, of course, but to take hold of it.

The gift is free but they must *'seek the Lord while he may be found'* (Isaiah 55:6). The way to obtain it is hedged about with opposition from enemies and friends, with thoughts of the cost, with false teachings and doubts about the truth.

In terms of the topics covered in this book, Christ gives a double warning: first against letting theoretical objections serve as an excuse for not returning to God and, secondly, against delaying your return.

Not to count the cost properly is foolish; not to return in time is disastrous. May I urge you, if you truly want to possess the salvation that Christ freely offers and that he alone can give, do not rest until you know that Christ is your Lord and Saviour, that your sins are forgiven, and that your place in God's kingdom is secure.

The assurance is quite clear. The blind men persevered and their sight was restored. Christ's words in Matthew 7:7-8 are equally definite:

'Ask and it will be given to you;
  seek and you will find;
  knock and the door will be opened to you.

[8] *For everyone who asks receives;*
  he who seeks finds;
  and to him who knocks, the door will be opened.'

Scripture Index

Also available on Amazon and other sellers:

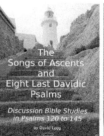

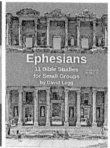
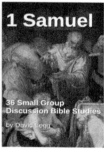

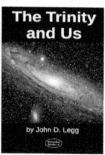

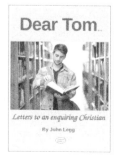
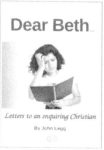
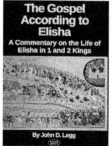

Printed in Great Britain
by Amazon

13497922R00059